Cooking with
COLORADO'S
GREATEST CHEFS

MARILYNN A. BOOTH

Photography by
JOHN FIELDER

Published by
WESTCLIFFE PUBLISHERS, INC.
ENGLEWOOD, COLORADO

Special thanks to Caren, Alison, Caleigh,
Laura, and Perri Forbes

EDITORS: Sandra J. Taylor, Suzanne Venino

DESIGN: Rebecca Finkel, F + P Graphic Design

PRODUCTION MANAGER: Suzanne Venino

INTERNATIONAL STANDARDS BOOK NUMBER
1-56579-127-4

LIBRARY OF CONGRESS CATALOGUE NUMBER
94-62204

PUBLISHED BY
Westcliffe Publishers, Inc.
2650 South Zuni Street
Englewood, Colorado 80110

PRINTED IN CHINA BY
Palace Press International

First Frontispiece: Indian paintbrush, Weminuche Wilderness
Second Frontispiece: Fresh snow on lodgepole pines, Arapaho National Forest
Third Frontispiece: Sunset over the Gore Range

Sunrise, San Juan Mountains

Everyday throughout the year these chefs create hundreds of dishes, under tremendous deadlines, while maintaining a standard of excellence deserving the highest possible ratings. They help us celebrate holidays, birthdays, marriages, anniversaries, graduations, promotions, retirements, and the joys of life. Thank you for all you have done and for all you will do to make each and every dining experience a memorable occasion.

AUGUSTA
Denver
   Roland Ulber

BEANO'S CABIN
Avon
   Joseph P. Keegan

THE BLACK BEAR INN
Lyons
   Hans J. Wyppler

THE BLACK SWAN
Englewood
   Niels van Leeuwen
   Frederick Clabaugh

THE BRIARWOOD INN
Golden
   Tom Morris

THE BRISTOL AT ARROWHEAD
Edwards
   Dennis B. Corwin

THE BROADMOOR
Colorado Springs
   Siegfried Eisenberger

CACHE CACHE
Aspen
   Michael W. Beary

CAMPAGNA
Telluride
   Vincent Esposito

C LAZY U RANCH
Granby
   Stephen Reynolds

CLIFF YOUNG'S
Denver
   Sean Brasel

EUROPEAN CAFE
Boulder and Denver
   Radek Cerny

FLAGSTAFF HOUSE
Boulder
   Mark Monette

THE FORT
Morrison
   Michael R. Barnett

THE HOME RANCH
Clark
   Clyde R. Nelson

THE IMPERIAL
Denver
   George Yu

KEYSTONE RANCH
Keystone
   Christopher Wing

KRABLOONIK
Snowmass Village
   John Roberts

LA MARMOTTE
Telluride
   Nöelle Lepel-Cointet

LA PETITE MAÍSON
Colorado Springs
   Holly B. Mervis

L'APOGÉE
Steamboat Springs
   Richard Billingham

LA RENAISSANCE
Pueblo
   Straud Fredregill
   Robert A. Fredregill

LE BOSQUET
Crested Butte
   Victor R. Shepard

THE LEFT BANK
Vail
   Luc Meyer

MIRABELLE AT BEAVER CREEK
Beaver Creek
   Daniel Joly

NORMANDY
Denver
   Robert Mancuso

PALACE ARMS
Denver
   Jeffrey L. Erickson

PICASSO
Edwards
   Fabrice Beaudoin

PIÑONS
Aspen
   Robert Mobilian

Q'S
Boulder
   John Platt

RENAISSANCE
Aspen
   Charles Dale

RESTAURANT AT THE LITTLE NELL
Aspen
   George Mahaffey

THE SAVOY
Berthoud
   Jean Martini

SOUPÇON
Crested Butte
   Mac Bailey

SWEET BASIL
Vail
   Thomas Salamunovich

TAKAH SUSHI
Aspen
   Kathy B. Sisson
   Johnie Mickles

TALL TIMBER
Durango
   Dennis J. Shakan

TANTE LOUISE
Denver
   Michael Degenhart

TERRA BISTRO
Vail
   Cynthia Walt

traMONTI
Beaver Creek
   Cynde Arnold

TUSCANY
Denver
   Tim A. Fields

240 UNION
Lakewood
   Matthew Franklin

THE WILDFLOWER
Vail
   James E. Cohen

ZENITH AMERICAN GRILL
Denver
   Kevin Taylor

EXECUTIVE CHEF FOR THE BOOK
   David Coder

In Memory of

Thomas W. Booth,

Father and Friend

Colorado columbines,
Rocky Mountain
National Park

ARTICHOKE BERNADINE

2 ounces cream cheese, softened
2 tablespoons milk
⅓ cup mayonnaise
¼ teaspoon dried dill
¼ clove garlic, minced
¼ teaspoon seasoned salt
¼ teaspoon pepper
1 14-ounce can artichoke hearts, drained and cut into pieces
1 2-ounce can roasted green chilies, drained and chopped
⅓ cup grated Cheddar cheese
¼ cup freshly grated Parmesan cheese
Toast points or crackers as accompaniment

PREPARATION

Preheat oven to 350 degrees. Combine cream cheese and milk, using a mixer, then blend in mayonnaise, dill, garlic, salt and pepper. Place artichoke pieces and green chilies in bottom of chafing dish. Pour cream cheese mixture on top and sprinkle with Cheddar and Parmesan cheeses. Bake until bubbly, 20–30 minutes. Serve with toast points or crackers.

NOTE

• Artichoke Bernadine can also be served as a vegetable side dish. We thought you would like it as an appetizer.

SERVES: 4
PREPARATION: 10 minutes
COOKING: 20–30 minutes

La Renaissance

La Renaissance
217 East Routt Avenue
Pueblo, Colorado 81004
(719) 543-6367

La Renaissance typifies casual, relaxed dining in a unique atmosphere. Located in a lovely old church built in 1888 with high, vaulted ceilings and stained-glass windows, La Renaissance offers seasonal delicacies combined with traditional cuisine to produce an exceptional dining experience.

STRAUD FREDREGILL

ROBERT A. FREDREGILL

Parry primrose, Rawah Wilderness

BUFFALO CARPACCIO WITH
MARINATED FENNEL AND ROASTED RED PEPPERS

Marinated Fennel

4 fennel bulbs, rinsed, trimmed, and cut in half lengthwise

2 cups chicken stock, or enough to cover fennel bulbs

1 tablespoon pickling spice

Marinated Roasted Red Peppers

4 red bell peppers

1 tablespoon olive oil

1 clove garlic, pressed

Salt and pepper to taste

Buffalo Carpaccio

12 ounces buffalo sirloin

Accompaniments

Olive oil to drizzle

Balsamic vinegar to drizzle

6–8 ounces Reggiano Parmesan cheese

Cracked black pepper

1 loaf french bread, thinly sliced and toasted

PREPARATION

1. Marinated Fennel. Place fennel halves in a saucepan, cover with chicken stock, add pickling spice, and bring to a boil. Remove from heat and refrigerate fennel and liquid for 24 hours. Slice when ready to serve.

2. Marinated Roasted Red Peppers. Roast red peppers on grill or under broiler until skins blister and blacken all over. Remove and discard peel, seeds, and membrane. Slice into thin strips and place in bowl. Add oil, garlic, salt and pepper. Mix thoroughly.

3. Buffalo Carpaccio. Cut buffalo sirloin across the grain into 16 very thin strips and pound with mallet.

4. Serving. Divide fennel among 4 plates, placing it at top of each plate. Arrange 4 buffalo strips at bottom, opposite fennel. Drizzle oil and vinegar around buffalo. Place 2 Parmesan curls *(see Note)* and roasted peppers between fennel and buffalo. Sprinkle with cracked black pepper. Place 4 slices of toasted bread on both sides of buffalo.

NOTE

• To make cheese curls, slice Parmesan cheese with cheese knife and roll up each slice to form a curl.

SERVES: 4

PREPARATION: 15–20 minutes
(fennel marinates overnight)

COOKING: 20–30 minutes

THE BROADMOOR

The Penrose Room
The Broadmoor
One Lake Avenue
Colorado Springs, Colorado 80906
(719) 634-7711

A grand resort hotel built in 1918, The Broadmoor reflects a legacy of elegance, impeccable service, and exquisite dining. The Penrose Room serves continental cuisine, prepared at tableside, and is truly worthy of its Mobil five-star and AAA five-diamond ratings.

SIEGFRIED EISENBERGER

CRAB CAKES WITH CHINESE FIVE SPICE AND GINGER-LIME AIOLI

Crab Cakes
¼ pound sea scallops
Pinch of salt
¼ cup heavy cream
1 egg white
1 pound lump crabmeat
2 tablespoons chopped fresh cilantro
2 tablespoons chopped fresh mint
3 tablespoons minced green scallions
1 teaspoon Chinese five spice
½ cup dry bread crumbs
2 tablespoons corn oil for sautéing

Ginger-Lime Aioli
2 egg yolks
1 tablespoon Dijon mustard
¼ cup fresh lime juice (about 6 limes)
1 tablespoon peeled, finely minced gingerroot
½ cup canola oil
Salt and pepper to taste

Garnish
1 cup field greens
Vinaigrette (optional)

PREPARATION

1. Crab Cakes. Place scallops in food processor or blender, add pinch of salt, and purée. With motor running, add cream in steady stream, then egg white. Transfer to bowl and gently fold in remaining ingredients, except bread crumbs and corn oil. Form into 8 cakes and lightly coat with bread crumbs. Refrigerate until ready to use.

When ready to serve, heat oil over medium-high heat in a large sauté pan. Sauté crab cakes until golden brown, about 5 minutes.

2. Ginger-Lime Aioli. Place egg yolks, mustard, lime juice, and gingerroot in food processor or blender and process 1 minute. Add canola oil very slowly at first, increasing as aioli thickens. If aioli becomes too thick, add a drop or so of water or more lime juice. Season with salt and pepper.

3. Serving. Toss field greens with your favorite vinaigrette or leave undressed. Arrange greens on each plate, top with two cakes per plate, and drizzle with aioli.

SERVES: 4
PREPARATION: 20 minutes
COOKING: 5 minutes

240 Union
240 Union Boulevard
Lakewood, Colorado 80228
(303) 989-3562

240 Union wins applause for "creative" new American fare. The contemporary, casual setting is first class, from patio to dining room. Enjoy roasted sea bass with black olive crust, lamb chops with rosemary mustard aioli, or gourmet pizza prepared in applewood-burning ovens.

MATTHEW FRANKLIN

DAL
(EAST INDIAN DIP)

1 cup split peas
1 cup lentils
4 cups water
2 teaspoons ground cumin
2 teaspoons ground coriander
1 cup chopped red onions
2 tablespoons chopped garlic
¼ cup olive oil
1 cup tightly packed fresh cilantro
Kosher salt
Ground chipolte pepper to taste

Accompaniments (see Serving)
1 loaf fresh bread and chili oil
8 soft tortillas and 1 large cucumber, thinly sliced

PREPARATION

1. Dal. Rinse and pick over split peas and lentils. Place in large pot, add water, and cook until soft, about 30 minutes. In small pan, toast cumin and coriander over low heat until aromatic. In separate pan, sauté onions and garlic in olive oil over medium heat until translucent.

Purée cilantro in food processor or blender until fine, scraping sides down frequently. Add split peas, lentils, onions, and garlic, and process until mixture forms smooth paste. Add more olive oil if necessary. Season with cumin, coriander, salt, and chipolte. (The chipolte is extremely spicy, so add it sparingly.)

2. Serving. The dal may be served two ways. First, as a dip with fresh bread and drizzled with chili oil. The other to spread a thin layer of dal over the entire surface of a tortilla and add sliced cucumbers. Roll up the tortilla and slice into bite-sized pieces.

SERVES: 8
PREPARATION: 15 minutes
COOKING: 30 minutes

Terra Bistro
352 East Meadow Drive
Vail, Colorado 81657
(970) 476-6836

Terra Bistro, located in the Vail Athletic Club, takes a holistic approach to dining, offering sophisticated international cuisine prepared with natural ingredients and specializing in free-range meats and poultry. Food is prepared to reduce fat content while maintaining flavor.

CYNTHIA WALT

SPINACH STRUDEL, CHANTERELLE BISQUE AND TOMATO RELISH

Spinach Strudel
1–2 tablespoons olive oil
1 pound spinach, cleaned
1 tablespoon minced shallots
1 tablespoon minced garlic
16 sheets filo dough
1 cup grated Asiago cheese
Salt and pepper to taste

Chanterelle Bisque
1 tablespoon butter or olive oil
½ pound chanterelle mushrooms,
    cleaned and halved
1 teaspoon minced shallots
2 cups unsalted chicken or
    vegetable stock
½ cup heavy cream
Salt and white pepper to taste

Tomato Relish
8 Roma tomatoes, peeled,
    seeded, and halved lengthwise
1 teaspoon minced shallots
½ teaspoon minced garlic
1 tablespoon chopped fresh parsley
1 tablespoon chopped fresh basil

SERVES: 6
PREPARATION: 30 minutes
COOKING: 10 minutes

Q's
The Hotel Boulderado
2115 13th Street
Boulder, Colorado 80302
(303) 442-4880

*Located on the mezzanine
of the historic Hotel Boulderado,
Q's serves contemporary American
cuisine featuring foods indigenous
to Colorado. An intimate atmosphere combined with unique
culinary creations makes this spot
one of the finest in the state.*

PREPARATION

1. Strudel. Preheat oven to 450 degrees. Heat ½ tablespoon oil in sauté pan, add spinach, shallots, garlic, and sear. Salt and pepper to taste, set aside to cool. Lay 2 sheets of filo on baking sheet and brush lightly with olive oil. Sprinkle each with Asiago cheese. Repeat until each has 4 layers of cheese and filo.

Divide spinach mixture into 4 equal parts and spread 1 part on each strudel. Repeat entire process once. Carefully roll up strudels, beginning with shorter side. (Can be made ahead to this point, cover with plastic wrap.) Slice each roll into 3 equal portions and bake for 10 minutes.

2. Chanterelle Bisque. In large sauté pan, heat oil or butter. Add mushrooms and shallots, and sauté until mushrooms begin to soften. Add stock and cook until liquid is reduced by half. (Can be made ahead to this point; to continue, reheat mixture.) Stir in cream, simmer for 5 minutes, and season with salt and white pepper.

3. Tomato Relish. Dice tomatoes into ½-inch pieces. Toss with remaining ingredients, mixing thoroughly.

4. Serving. Spoon pool of chanterelle bisque onto each plate, place strudel in center, and top with tomato relish.

JOHN PLATT

MEADOW LAMB WITH TOMATO RELISH, WILTED CHARD AND WINTER SQUASH GRIDDLE CAKES

Tomato Relish
6 Roma tomatoes
1 tablespoon honey
1 teaspoon ground allspice
1 teaspoon champagne vinegar
Pinch of salt (optional)

Winter Squash Griddle Cakes
1 cup cooked butternut squash
1 egg
½ cup all-purpose flour
1 tablespoon butter
¼ teaspoon baking powder
½ teaspoon ground nutmeg
½ teaspoon salt
Dash of Tabasco
¼ teaspoon white pepper
Cornmeal for dusting
Olive oil for sautéing

Lamb
2 pounds lamb loin, fat and skin removed
½ cup Dijon mustard
½ cup bread crumbs
Olive oil

Wilted Chard
1 tablespoon olive oil
2 cups chopped Swiss chard
½ teaspoon minced garlic
1 orange, zest and juice
Pinch of salt (optional)

SERVES: 6
PREPARATION: 35 minutes
COOKING: 20 minutes

KEYSTONE RANCH

Keystone Ranch
1239 Keystone Ranch Road
Keystone, Colorado 80435
(970) 468-4130

The Keystone Ranch is rich in history of the Old West. Ute and Arapaho Indians used the area as their summer campground. Today, guests dine on elegant regional cuisine while seated in a log cabin with views of the Ten Mile and Gore Ranges.

PREPARATION

1. Tomato Relish. Bring medium-sized pan of water to a boil, add tomatoes, and remove when skins begin to separate. Peel, seed, and cut into slivers. Mix with remaining relish ingredients, add salt if necessary, and refrigerate.

2. Squash Griddlecakes. Mash squash in a medium bowl, mix with remaining ingredients, except cornmeal and oil. Shape into 12 1-inch patties, dust with cornmeal, and sauté in small amount of oil until golden brown.

3. Lamb. Brush lamb with mustard and coat with bread crumbs. Sauté in small amount of oil until medium rare, about 15 minutes. Slice into 12 pieces.

4. Wilted Chard. Heat oil and sauté all ingredients until chard wilts. Add salt if necessary.

5. Serving. Place 2 griddle cakes on each plate. Top with small amount of chard and two pieces of lamb. Spoon relish over half of each piece of lamb.

CHRISTOPHER WING

PAN-SEARED THAI BEEF WITH WATERCRESS SALAD, SPICY ONIONS AND PEANUT SAUCE

SERVES: 8
PREPARATION: 40 minutes
COOKING: 25 minutes

Piñons

Piñons
105 South Mill Street
Aspen, Colorado 81611
(970) 920-2021

Surrounded by turn-of-the-century paintings depicting the Wild West, diners are treated to "American cuisine with a Colorado touch." Patrons have been known to fly across the country for the elegant food expertly prepared by Chef Rob Mobilian.

Robert Mobilian

ROBERT MOBILIAN

Thai Spice
1 tablespoon garlic powder
1 tablespoon chili powder
1 tablespoon white pepper
1 tablespoon black pepper
1 tablespoon cayenne pepper

Peanut Sauce
¼ cup olive oil
1 teaspoon curry
1½ cups ground peanuts
1 teaspoon minced garlic
½ cup chicken stock
1 teaspoon Thai spice
1 cup coconut milk
½ teaspoon salt
1 tablespoon sugar
1 lemon, juice only

Watercress Salad
¼ cup rice vinegar
¼ cup peanut oil
2 tablespoons sesame oil
1 teaspoon minced shallots
1 teaspoon minced garlic
¼ cup Tamari sauce
1 tablespoon chopped fresh cilantro
1 tablespoon lime juice
Salt and pepper to taste
4 bunches watercress, cleaned

Spicy Onions
½ cup all-purpose flour
1 tablespoon paprika
2 teaspoons Thai spice
1 large red onion, thinly sliced
½ cup buttermilk
Peanut oil for frying

Beef
1 pound beef tenderloin
Olive oil for sautéing

PREPARATION

1. Thai Spice. Combine all ingredients in small bowl.

2. Peanut Sauce. Mix all ingredients in saucepan and simmer for 15 minutes. Keep warm.

3. Salad. Mix together flour, paprika and 2 teaspoons Thai spice. Soak onions in buttermilk, then toss in flour mixture. Fry in peanut oil until golden brown and set aside.

4. Spicy Onions. Mix rice wine vinegar, peanut oil, sesame oil, shallots, garlic, Tamari, cilantro, and lime juice. Salt and pepper to taste. Toss with cleaned watercress.

5. Beef. Cut beef into 8 2-ounce portions and dredge in remaining Thai spice. Heat olive oil over high heat, add beef, and sear on both sides until rare or medium-rare. Cut each piece into 4 slices.

6. Serving. Place salad in middle of plate, top with onions, drizzle peanut sauce on plate, and fan beef slices around salad.

Salmon Stuffed
with Mussels and Shrimp

Salmon

1 pound fresh salmon filet, in one piece

4 tablespoons salt

2 tablespoons brown sugar

½ tablespoon crushed black peppercorns

1 tablespoon crushed coriander

3 tablespoons chopped fresh baby dill

1 lemon

2 tablespoons virgin olive oil

Mussels and Shrimp Filling and Sauce

2 pounds fresh mussels

1 cup white wine

1 cup heavy cream

1 tablespoon chopped fresh tarragon

Salt and white pepper to taste

½ cup virgin olive oil

½ pound fresh shrimp,
    peeled and deveined

1 lemon, juice only

2 scallions, cut in long strips

SERVES: 4

PREPARATION: 45 minutes
(salmon sits 24 hours)

COOKING: 15 minutes

La Marmotte
150 West San Juan Avenue
Telluride, Colorado 81435
(970) 728-6232

*Hosts Bertrand Marchal and
Noelle Lepel-Cointet transport
France to the San Juan
Mountains. At La Marmotte
guests dine on outstanding
classic and regional French
cuisine. A romantic, cozy
restaurant, it is an ideal place
to linger over excellent wines
in an unhurried, civilized oasis
away from life's daily stresses.*

PREPARATION

1. Salmon. The day before serving, cover salmon with mixture of salt, brown sugar, pepper, coriander, and baby dill. Squeeze lemon juice over salmon and lightly brush with olive oil. Wrap salmon in plastic wrap and place heavy object, such as a pan or large book, on top of salmon. Refrigerate for 24 hours.

2. Mussels and Shrimp Filling and Sauce. The day of serving, scrub mussels and remove beards. Pour wine in large pan, add mussels, and cook over medium heat until mussels open. Remove mussels from liquid and set aside; return pan to stove. Continue cooking until liquid is reduced by half; add cream and reduce again by half. Add ½ tablespoon tarragon, season with salt and white pepper, and chill. This becomes the sauce.

Remove mussels from their shells, discarding any which did not open, and refrigerate until ready to use. Heat small amount of olive oil in sauté pan, add shrimp, and cook until they turn pink. Place in bowl and chill. When cool, mix shrimp, mussels, lemon juice, remaining olive, and remaining tarragon. Season with salt and pepper.

3. Serving. Thinly slice salmon. Spoon 2 tablespoons of mussel-shrimp mixture in middle of salmon and roll up. On individual serving plates, place equal amounts of sauce, arrange salmon in center, and garnish with scallions.

NOTES

- The salmon can also be served on toast points.
- For those on restricted diets, 2% milk can be substituted for heavy cream.

NOËLLE LEPEL-COINTET

TEQUILA MARINATED PRAWNS WITH LIME-CILANTRO SAUCE, CORN CAKES AND GRILLED RED & YELLOW PEPPERS

SERVES: 6
PREPARATION: 20 minutes
COOKING: 20 minutes

The Black Swan
200 Inverness Drive West
Englewood, Colorado 80112
(303) 799-5800

The Black Swan, rated four-diamonds by AAA, offers exceptional international cuisine. Enjoy a relaxed yet elegant atmosphere where service is paramount. The Black Swan is perfect for an intimate rendezvous or a serious business dinner.

NIELS VAN LEEUWEN

FREDERICK CLABAUGH

Tequila Marinade
1 cup tequila
2 tablespoons Vietnamese chili paste
 or garlic chili paste *(see Notes)*
4 tablespoons olive oil
1 tablespoon chopped yellow onion
2 limes, juice only
Pinch of salt and pepper

Prawns
18 prawns (jumbo shrimp),
 peeled and deveined

Grilled Peppers
1 yellow bell pepper
1 red bell pepper

Lime–Cilantro Sauce
½ tablespoon butter or olive oil
1 shallot, minced
2 limes, juice only
3 cups white wine
¾ cup unsalted butter, cut into pieces
1 tablespoon chopped fresh cilantro
Salt and pepper to taste

Corn Cakes
1 cup all-purpose flour
2 tablespoons cornmeal
1 egg
1 tablespoon chopped fresh cilantro
2 jalapeño peppers, seeded and diced
1 tablespoon chopped green onion
1 ear fresh corn, cut from cob
1 teaspoon baking soda
1 cup milk

PREPARATION

1. Tequila Marinade. Mix all ingredients in a glass bowl. Add shrimp and marinate for 15–20 minutes.

2. Prawns. Immediately prior to serving, grill shrimp for 3–4 minutes per side.

3. Grilled Peppers. Roast peppers over gas flame, on grill, or under broiler until charred. Remove and discard peel, seeds, and membrane. Cut into julienne strips.

4. Lime-Cilantro Sauce. Heat ½ tablespoon butter or olive oil in a saucepan. Add shallots and sauté until soft. Add lime juice and wine, and cook until reduced by three fourths. Add butter very slowly, whisking continually. Stir in cilantro. Salt and pepper to taste.

5. Corn Cakes. Combine all ingredients (mixture should resemble pancake batter). Heat large, lightly oiled sauté pan over medium heat and ladle batter into pan, creating 3-inch-diameter cakes. Cook until golden brown, approximately 1 minute per side.

6. Serving. Place sauce in center of each plate, top with corn cake, arrange 3 shrimp on each corn cake, and garnish with roasted peppers.

NOTES

   • Vietnamese chili paste and garlic chili paste can be found in most health food stores, Oriental markets, and large grocery store chains. Other red chili pastes can be substituted for the Vietnamese paste.

   • For those on restricted diets, the lime-cilantro sauce can be modified in two ways. One is to substitute margarine for the butter. The other is to make a wine reduction sauce. Follow the original instructions but reduce the wine by only half, omit the butter, then add remaining ingredients. This will have a stronger flavor than the butter sauce.

Autumn aspen grove, Sneffels Range   21

SALMON AND CUCUMBER TARTAR WITH WASABI OIL AND CRISPY NORI

SERVES: 8

PREPARATION: 30 minutes
(oil sits for one hour)

Sweet Basil
193 East Gore Creek Drive
Vail, Colorado 81657
(970) 476-0125

Sweet Basil features imaginative American cuisine with Mediterranean and Asian influences. The menu, which changes frequently, remains true to each season. Sweet Basil's primary goal is to create food that excites the palate, is visually arresting, and leaves a lasting impression.

Thomas Salamunovit

THOMAS SALAMUNOVICH

Wasabi Oil
⅓ cup peanut oil
1 ½ tablespoons wasabi paste *(see Note)*
1 1-inch piece gingerroot, peeled and chopped
2 stalks lemon grass *(see Note)*

Crispy Nori
4 sheets nori *(see Note)*
1 tablespoon water
2 tablespoons rice flour
Oil for deep frying

Seasoned Salt
1 tablespoon black sesame seeds *(see Note)*
2 tablespoons bonito flakes *(see Note)*
½ teaspoon kosher salt

Dressing
1 tablespoon lime juice
1 tablespoon soy sauce
1 tablespoon rice vinegar

Salmon and Cucumber Tartar
1 ½ pounds salmon, cleaned and finely diced
1 English cucumber, diced
4 ounces daikon root, peeled and diced
2 shallots, diced

Garnish
1 English cucumber, thinly sliced
2 red radishes, thinly sliced

PREPARATION

1. Wasabi Oil. Mix all ingredients in a small pan and steep over medium heat for 5 minutes. Remove from stove and let sit for 1 hour in warm place. Strain.

2. Nori. Cut nori sheets into 32 equal triangles. Mix water and rice flour in small bowl and brush over one side of each triangle. Heat oil until hot and deep fry each piece until crispy, approximately 45 seconds. Transfer to paper towels.

3. Seasoned Salt. Heat small sauté pan, add sesame seeds and toast, being careful not to burn seeds. Grind seeds with bonito flakes and salt.

4. Dressing. Combine all ingredients in small bowl.

5. Salmon and Cucumber Tartar. Combine salmon, cucumber, daikon root, and shallot in bowl. Add three fourths of infused oil and three fourths of seasoned salt and mix. Add three fourths of dressing, blend well.

6. Serving. Fan cucumber into a circle on 8 plates, leaving a 3-inch hole in center. Alternate every third slice with a sliced radish. Divide salmon tartar into 8 equal portions and place in center of each plate. Sprinkle remaining dressing onto circle of cucumbers. Repeat with remaining infused oil and seasoned salt. Position nori triangles around salmon.

NOTE

• Wasabi paste, nori (seaweed), bonito flakes, lemon grass, and black sesame seeds can be found in Oriental markets, specialty stores, and many health food stores. The ingredients can also be ordered from large grocery store chains.

SHIITAKE MUSHROOMS, THYME AND WALNUT HANDROLLS

Shiitake, Thyme and Walnut Filling
1 tablespoon olive oil
8 ounces shiitake mushrooms, sliced
1 teaspoon low-sodium soy sauce
1 lemon, juice only
White pepper to taste
2 teaspoons fresh thyme leaves, stems removed
½ cup coarsely chopped walnuts

Sushi Rice
1 cup Japanese rice, medium grain
2 teaspoons salt
1 tablespoon sugar
3 tablespoons rice vinegar

Handroll
4 sheets nori *(see Note)*
Wasabi paste

PREPARATION

1. Shiitake, Thyme and Walnut Filling. Heat olive oil in heavy-bottomed, high-walled skillet until oil smokes. Add shiitakes and sauté until golden brown. Stir in soy sauce and lemon juice, season with white pepper and cook until almost all liquid has evaporated. Add thyme and walnuts and set aside to cool.

2. Sushi Rice. Cook rice according to package instructions. Measure 2 cups and save remainder for another use. Return rice to pan but do not heat. Dissolve salt and sugar in vinegar and add to rice, using rubber spatula to flake rice and break up lumps.

3. Handrolls. Lay nori on flat, dry surface. With moist hands, spread one fourth of rice lengthwise along one end of nori sheet; rice should cover approximately one fourth to one third of sheet. Spread a line of wasabi down center and top with one fourth of shiitake mixture. Roll up, beginning with rice end. Pat loose edges with a little rice.

4. Serving. Cut each roll into pieces and place on individual plates.

NOTE
• Nori and wasabi paste can be found in most health food stores, Oriental markets and some large grocery store chains.

SERVES: 4
PREPARATION: 15–20 minutes
COOKING: 25–30 minutes

たか
TAKAH SUSHI

Takah Sushi
420 East Hyman Avenue
Aspen, Colorado 81611
(970) 925-8588

Takah Sushi features Japanese-accented cuisine ranging from Tamari-glazed swordfish to vegetarian sushi rolls. Patrons marvel at the skill and art of sushi preparation while enjoying delectable, exquisitely presented creations.

JOHNIE MICKLES

LOBSTER QUESADILLA WITH FRESH PINEAPPLE SALSA

SERVES: 4
PREPARATION: 30 minutes
COOKING: 5 minutes

The Bristol at Arrowhead
Country Club of the Rockies
676 Sawatch Drive
Edwards, Colorado 81632
(970) 926-2111

*Nationally acclaimed,
The Bristol at Arrowhead is
located in the Country Club
of the Rockies and is open to
the public for fine dining.
Featuring creative American
cuisine, gracious service, and a
magnificent setting, The Bristol
offers something for everyone.*

Pineapple Salsa
½ medium pineapple, peeled,
    cored, and diced; reserve juice
1 red bell pepper, diced
3 scallions, diced
1 Anaheim chili, diced
3 tablespoons chopped fresh cilantro
1 tablespoon fresh lime juice
½ teaspoon salt (optional)

Lobster Filling
8 corn tortillas
1 teaspoon puréed chipolte chili
3 ounces each, grated Monterey Jack,
    white Cheddar, and Havarti cheeses
4 ounces cooked lobster
    (may use canned)
4 scallions, diced
1¼ teaspoons olive oil
½ cup sour cream (optional)

PREPARATION

1. Salsa. Mix all ingredients in a medium-sized glass bowl, including reserved pineapple juice. Cover and let stand at room temperature for 1 hour.

2. Lobster Quesadilla. Brush 4 tortillas with puréed chipolte chili. (These chilies are very hot: ¼ teaspoon per tortilla is generally enough for those who like very spicy dishes. If you prefer a milder flavor, reduce amount to ⅛ teaspoon.)

Combine cheeses, divide into 4 equal portions, and sprinkle over each of the 4 tortillas. Then sprinkle with lobster and scallions and place remaining 4 tortillas on top and press down lightly.

Heat ¼ teaspoon olive oil in large skillet and add one quesadilla. Cook over medium to medium-low heat until golden brown on both sides. Transfer to cutting board and pat with paper towel to absorb excess oil. Cut into quarters. Repeat with remaining quesadillas, adding olive oil as needed.

3. Serving. To decorate quesadillas, put sour cream in a squeeze bottle and draw tic-tac-toe pattern on each. Place pineapple salsa in middle of each plate and arrange quesadilla quarters around salsa.

NOTES

• This salsa makes a wonderful topping for grilled fish. For an Oriental version, substitute rice vinegar for lime juice, add 1 teaspoon sesame oil, and grated ginger to taste.

• Crab or shrimp may be used instead of lobster in the quesadillas.

DENNIS B. CORWIN

Fennel Bulb with Parmesan Cheese, Italian Parsley and Olive Oil

1 large fennel bulb
⅓ pound Reggiano Parmesan cheese
32 fresh Italian parsley leaves
Fresh ground black pepper
Tuscan extra-virgin olive oil

Preparation

Discard green top by cutting just above bulb, slice bulb very thinly from top to bottom. Do not cut from side to side, for that will create pieces instead of slices. The object is to create whole, thin slices of fennel. Cut cheese into thin slices.

Serving. Place single fennel slice on each plate and cover with single slice of cheese. Place approximately 8 parsley leaves on each piece of cheese and grind pepper over salad. Drizzle with olive oil, making sure not to soak the mixture with too much oil. Serve immediately.

Notes

• The quality of the ingredients is essential to making this an outstanding dish. Substituting other cheeses for the Reggiano will alter the flavor. The same is true for the Tuscan olive oil.

• Round, fat fennel bulbs will be the sweetest.

• This recipe should not be done ahead of time, or the fennel will brown and the cheese will dry out.

SERVES: 3–4
PREPARATION: 5 minutes

Campagna
435 West Pacific Avenue
Telluride, Colorado 81435
(970) 728-6190

Campagna serves country food from Tuscany, the heart of northern Italy. Using only the finest ingredients, Chef-owner Vincent Esposito prepares food that Bon Appetit *magazine has called "sophisticated yet homey." You'll feel like you stepped into a Tuscan country home.*

VINCENT ESPOSITO

Meadow, South Park

RED COOKED DUCK SPRING ROLL
WITH SAMBAL RISOTTO AND BABY GREENS

SERVES: 6

PREPARATION: 1 hour
(duck marinates overnight)

COOKING: 1 hour

THE LITTLE NELL

Restaurant at The Little Nell
The Little Nell
675 East Durant Street
Aspen, Colorado 81611
(970) 920-4600

The Restaurant at The Little Nell combines European ambiance with a Rocky Mountain setting—the ultimate mountain getaway. Chef George Mahaffey mixes regional ingredients with exotic flavors, creating dishes that have won the restaurant Mobil's four-star and AAA's four-diamond awards.

GEORGE MAHAFFEY

Red Cooked Duck

1 duck breast, skinned
  (approximately 6 ounces)
1 tablespoon sesame oil
¼ cup sherry
¼ cup soy sauce
1 tablespoon sliced garlic
2 tablespoons chopped scallions
1 teaspoon sambal paste *(see Notes)*
1 tablespoon sliced gingerroot
1 cup chicken stock
2 pieces star anise

Sauce

Reserved duck marinade
2 tablespoons rice vinegar
2 tablespoons maple syrup
1 teaspoon cornstarch

Baby Greens

1 cup mixed baby lettuce
2 tablespoons each,
  julienned red and yellow bell peppers
2 tablespoons chive pieces,
  cut 2 inches long
2 tablespoons julienned jicama
2 tablespoons fried rice noodles
2 tablespoons vinaigrette
Salt and pepper to taste

Spring Rolls

¼ cup virgin peanut oil, cold pressed
4 tablespoons julienned carrots
4 tablespoons julienned snow peas
½ cup sliced white onions,
  cut from center
1 teaspoon chopped garlic
1 teaspoon freshly grated gingerroot
1 cup julienned Naja cabbage
3 tablespoons chopped cashews
3 sheets spring-roll wrappers, 7-inch size

Sambal Risotto

3 cups unsalted chicken stock
¼ cup coconut milk
1 tablespoon minced shallots
1 tablespoon sambal paste
2 tablespoons butter
4 tablespoons sliced mushrooms
2 tablespoons sliced snow peas
½ cup arborio rice
1 tablespoon each
  chopped fresh basil and cilantro,
  mixed together

PREPARATION

1. Red Cooked Duck. Grill or broil duck until rare. Combine remaining ingredients in saucepan and bring to a boil. Simmer for 10 minutes, then remove from heat. Place duck in marinade and refrigerate overnight. Remove duck and set aside, reserving marinate for sauce.

2. Sauce. Combine reserved marinade, rice vinegar, and maple syrup in saucepan and bring to boil. In bowl, mix cornstarch with 1 tablespoon sauce, stirring until smooth. Return mixture to saucepan and whisk to blend. When sauce thickens, remove from heat and strain. Cool to room temperature.

3. Baby Greens. Combine all ingredients and season with salt and pepper.

4. Spring Rolls. Heat skillet until very hot, add peanut oil, carrots, snow peas, and onions, and stir-fry for 30 seconds. Add garlic, gingerroot, and cabbage, and stir-fry for another 45 seconds. Remove from heat and spread mixture onto cookie sheet. Allow to cool completely.

Dice duck, mix with cashews and stir-fried vegetables. Divide mixture into 3 equal portions and place in center of 3 spring-roll wrappers. Roll tightly according to package directions. (Spring rolls can be made ahead to this point but should be covered with damp towel until ready to use.)

Fry spring rolls in 350 degree oil until golden. Drain well. Slice off ends, then cut spring rolls in half diagonally.

5. Sambal Risotto. Combine chicken stock, coconut milk, shallots, and sambal in saucepan, bring to a boil, then set aside. In separate pan, melt butter, add mushrooms and snow peas, and sauté for 30 seconds. Add rice, stirring until mixed. Add half the chicken stock mixture and simmer for 10 minutes, stirring continually. As liquid is absorbed, add more stock mixture until it is incorporated and rice is creamy but still retains its shape. Stir in basil and cilantro and serve immediately.

6. Serving. Place spring-roll halves in center of each plate. Spoon an equal amount of sambal risotto next to spring roll and garnish with baby greens. Finish by drizzling 2 tablespoons of sauce around each plate.

NOTES

• Sambal paste is an Indonesian chili paste that can be found in specialty grocery stores and Oriental markets. The most common brand is Sambal Oeleck.

• The spring rolls can be served without frying for those who are on restricted diets.

• Sambal risotto is also good with Indonesian chicken and fish dishes.

SMOKED TROUT, POTATO AND ZUCCHINI CAKE, ONION MARMALADE AND CHIVE CREAM

SERVES: 6

PREPARATION: 15 minutes
(30 minutes to cool)

COOKING: 30 minutes

Q's
The Hotel Boulderado
2115 13th Street
Boulder, Colorado 80302
(303) 442-4880

Located on the mezzanine of the historic Hotel Boulderado, Q's serves contemporary American cuisine featuring foods indigenous to Colorado. An intimate atmosphere combined with unique culinary creations makes this spot one of the finest in the state.

Onion Marmalade
2 large red onions, chopped
1 cup red wine vinegar
1 cup Zinfandel wine
1 cup brown sugar
2 bay leaves
1 tablespoon black pepper

Chive Cream
1 cup sour cream or crème fraîche
¼ cup chopped fresh chives

Potato and Zucchini Cake
2 russet potatoes, peeled and grated
1 zucchini, grated
1 egg
¼ cup all-purpose flour
Salt and white pepper to taste
1–2 tablespoons olive oil for sautéing

Trout
1 pound smoked trout

PREPARATION

1. Onion Marmalade. Place all ingredients in non-reactive saucepan and simmer until liquid is almost gone and mixture is a dark syrup. Flavor should be balanced between tart and sweet; adjust with vinegar or sugar if necessary. Discard bay leaves and set aside to cool. (This can be made ahead.)

2. Chive Cream. Mix sour cream or crème fraîche with chives and set aside.

3. Potato and Zucchini Cake. Combine potatoes, zucchini, egg, and flour in large bowl. Season with salt and pepper. Heat 1 tablespoon oil, place 3 tablespoons cake mixture in hot oil, and flatten to ½-inch thickness. Cook over medium-high heat until golden brown and crisp on both sides. Transfer to paper towels to absorb excess oil. Repeat to make a total of 6 cakes.

4. Trout. Divide trout into 6 equal portions.

5. Serving. Place 1 potato and zucchini cake on each plate, top with 1 tablespoon marmalade, add trout and a dollop of chive cream.

NOTE

• For those on restricted diets, use 2 egg whites instead of 1 egg, omit the sour cream or crème fraîche, and top with chopped chives.

JOHN PLATT

Opposite: Cascade Creek, San Juan Mountains
Overleaf: Sunset, Gore Range

MEDITERRANEAN VEGETABLE SOUP

¼ pound butter

½ onion, rough cut

1 tablespoon chopped garlic

1 green bell pepper, rough cut

½ pound fresh tomatoes

5 ounces tomato paste

6 cups water

1 yellow squash, rough cut

1 zucchini, rough cut

1 stalk celery, rough cut

1 carrot, rough cut

½ eggplant, peeled and rough cut

1 ½ potatoes, peeled and rough diced

1 tablespoon chopped fresh basil

Salt and pepper to taste

SERVES: 8

PREPARATION: 30 minutes

COOKING: 2 hours

The Savoy
535 Third Street
Berthoud, Colorado 80513
(970) 532-4095

From the moment you enter

The Savoy you are immersed

in a French-country atmosphere.

Owner Chantal Martini serves

Contential-French cuisine

expertly prepared and presented

by Chef Jean Martini. The Savoy

is the perfect spot to celebrate

any occasion.

PREPARATION

Melt butter in large soup pot, add onions, garlic, bell peppers, and sauté until soft. Add tomatoes and cook for 5 minutes. Stir in tomato paste and water. Add remaining ingredients, except salt and pepper. Bring to a boil, then reduce heat and simmer over low heat for 2 hours. Season with salt and pepper.

NOTE

• The soup is best when made a day ahead. It also freezes well.

JEAN MARTINI

CIDER AND ONION SOUP
WITH SMOKED MOZZARELLA CROUTONS

MAKES: 1½ gallons
PREPARATION: 20 minutes
COOKING: 4 hours

krabloonik

Krabloonik
4250 Divide Road
Snowmass Village, Colorado 81615
(970) 923-4342

At Krabloonik, home to the world's largest husky kennel, guests can tour the kennels or experience the thrill of a dog sled ride before dining on wild game specialties. A log cabin with sunken fire pit, the Krabloonik provides a relaxed, elegant location for a true Colorado experience.

JOHN ROBERTS

Pheasant Stock
3 carrots, peeled and rough cut
1 white onion, rough cut
½ bunch celery, rough cut
1 pheasant, bones only *(see Note)*
2½ gallons cold water

Cider and Onions
4 white onions, sliced into circles
¾ cup brown sugar
½ cup Calvados
2 tablespoons apple cider vinegar
4 cups apple cider
Salt and pepper to taste

Smoked Mozzarella Croutons
1 loaf French bread baguette,
    cut into ½-inch slices
¼ cup olive oil
1 pound smoked mozzarella, grated

PREPARATION

1. Pheasant Stock. Preheat oven to 450 degrees. Debone pheasant, saving meat for another occasion. Place carrots, onions, celery, and pheasant bones in roasting pan and bake until golden brown. Transfer to stock pot and add cold water. Bring to a boil, reduce heat, and simmer until reduced to 1½ gallons. Be sure to skim any fat or scum that rises to top. Strain and return to stock pot.

2. Cider and Onions. Heat sauté pan over very high heat, add onions and reduce heat. As onions begin to soften, add brown sugar and continue to cook, stirring frequently, until caramelized, approximately 1 hour. Add Calvados and ignite by touching a match to pan but be very careful for flames can be high. Stir in vinegar. Transfer to pheasant stock, add cider and bring to a boil. Reduce heat to medium-low and cook for 30 minutes. Season with salt and pepper.

3. Croutons. Preheat oven to 350 degrees. Place sliced bread on cookie sheet, brush with olive oil, and top with generous amount of cheese. Bake until cheese is bubbling.

4. Serving. Pour soup into individual bowls and top each with a crouton.

NOTE

• The pheasant meat can be used in Cornish Game Hen with Pheasant Sausage Stuffing and Red Onion Marmalade (page 93) or may be frozen for later use.

SPLIT PEA CONSOMMÉ

Split Pea Broth

1 tablespoon olive oil

1 ½ cups finely diced carrots

1 ½ cups finely diced celery

1 ½ cups finely diced onions

½ pound andouille sausage

18 ounces split peas,
    rinsed and picked over

1 ¼ gallons (6 quarts) chicken stock

½ cup butter

3 smoked ham hocks

1 ½ bay leaves

1 carrot, julienned for garnish

Clarifying Ingredients

1 pound boneless, skinless chicken

8 egg whites

½ cup chopped tomatoes

1 bay leaf

6 peppercorns

1 sprig thyme

SERVES: 8

PREPARATION: 15 minutes
(chill for 4 hours)

COOKING: 3 hours

Normandy
1515 Madison Street
Denver, Colorado 80206
(303) 321-3311

*Walking into the Normandy
is entering a world of simple
elegance. Antique leaded-glass
windows and period furniture
make this restored turn-of-the-
century home the perfect location
for Chef Robert Mancuso, a
member of Culinary Team
USA, to create award-winning
French dishes.*

PREPARATION

1. Split Pea Broth. Heat olive oil in large soup pot, add diced carrots, celery, onions, and sausage and sauté until vegetables are soft. Add remaining ingredients, except julienned carrot, reduce heat, and simmer until peas are tender, about 2–2½ hours. Strain and cool at room temperature for approximately 4 hours.

2. Clarifying Ingredients. The following process is used to clear broth of impurities. Grind chicken in food processor. Mix with egg whites and add to broth along with remaining ingredients. Return to stove and heat over medium-high heat, stirring occasionally, until broth reaches 135–140 degrees; the liquid will look frothy. Stop stirring and allow "raft" to form. A raft is a filter of clarifying ingredients and impurities that looks like foam. Be very careful not to disturb raft, other than directed, or broth will become cloudy.

Lower a soup ladle through raft into broth to make a hole, either on a side or in center. The hole will allow broth to simmer. Reduce heat and gently simmer for 20–30 minutes. Do not let boil. At the end of cooking, the raft will be fairly solid and broth will have cleared.

3. Serving. Line fine mesh strainer with cheese cloth or coffee filter, ladle consommé into strainer, and let strain slowly. The raft pieces will break apart and be caught in strainer. Pour consommé into individual bowls and garnish with julienned carrots.

ROBERT MANCUSO

This recipe is an adaptation of the Culinary Team USA's Hot Essence of Split Pea. For more information about the team and their recipes, please contact the American Culinary Federation, 10 San Bartola Road, St. Augustine, Florida 32086

COLORADO SUNSET SOUP WITH RED & YELLOW PEPPERS AND SMOKED GULF SHRIMP

SERVES: 6
PREPARATION: 15 minutes
COOKING: 15 minutes

TUSCANY

Tuscany
Loews Giorgio Hotel
4150 East Mississippi Avenue
Denver, Colorado 80222
(303) 782-9300

With fresh-cut flowers, marble fireplace, and an evening harpist, the Tuscany is the perfect setting for dining on an exquisitely prepared Italian cuisine. The award-winning menu is complemented by a large selection of Italian wines. Tuscany is ideal for celebrating any occasion—or creating one.

Sunset Soup
1 large yellow onion, rough cut
2 garlic cloves, rough cut
6 cups unsalted chicken stock, hot
4 cups heavy cream
10 sprigs fresh cilantro
1 cup all-purpose flour
1 pound unsalted butter
8 red bell peppers, rough cut
8 yellow bell peppers, rough cut
Salt and pepper to taste

Smoked Shrimp
6 large shrimp, peeled and deveined
Hickory chips

Garnish
3 tablespoons finely chopped
 fresh cilantro

PREPARATION

1. Sunset Soup. In this recipe, two identical soups are made and then combined when served, so begin by dividing in half the quantities given for onions, garlic, chicken stock, cream, cilantro sprigs, flour, and butter. In one saucepan, place the red peppers; in another, the yellow peppers. Sauté each with half the butter, onions, and garlic until onions are soft. Sprinkle each with half the flour and sauté for 3 minutes. Add half the chicken stock, cream, and cilantro to each pot, and simmer for 5 more minutes. Purée each soup separately in a blender for 5 minutes.

2. Smoked Shrimp. Soak hickory chips in water for 30 minutes. Heat a cast-iron skillet over very high heat, and when hot, add hickory chips. Cover skillet with screen or small grill and place shrimp on top. Cover with bowl and smoke for 5 minutes. Remove shrimp and slice in half.

3. Serving. Simultaneously ladle equal portions of red soup and yellow soup into bowl. Half will be red; half yellow. Pass a knife slowly from red to yellow, creating a few spikes (or mountains). Place two shrimp halves in yellow portion of soup (clouds). In red section, make a cactus with chopped cilantro.

NOTES

• The shrimp can be smoked over 3 or 4 rosemary sprigs instead of hickory chips. Both methods create a lot of smoke. An alternative is grilling.

• For those on dietary restrictions, substitute margarine for butter, or use 1–2 tablespoons olive oil. Substitute 2% milk for heavy cream.

TIM A. FIELDS

CORN CHOWDER WITH
LOBSTER, MUSSELS AND SWEET PEPPERS

SERVES: 8
PREPARATION: 15 minutes
COOKING: 45 minutes

Flagstaff House

Flagstaff House
1138 Flagstaff Road
Boulder, Colorado 80302
(303) 442-4640

Flagstaff House, built in 1929 as a mountain cabin over-looking Boulder, is a Mobil four-star, AAA four-diamond, and The Wine Spectator *magazine's grand award-winning restaurant. Owned and operated by Don Monette and his sons Mark and Scott, Flagstaff House is renowned for its innovative dishes and extensive wine cellar.*

2 cups white wine
3 cloves garlic, chopped
1 onion, chopped
15 peppercorns
1 sprig fresh thyme
1 bay leaf
3 pounds mussels, scrubbed
    and beards removed
Pinch of saffron
2 cups fish stock *(see Note)*
1 cup fresh corn
1 quart cream
2 tablespoons butter
½ cup chopped lobster meat
1 red bell pepper, diced
1 yellow bell pepper, diced
Salt and pepper to taste

PREPARATION

In large pot, bring wine, garlic, onions, peppercorns, thyme, and bay leaf to a boil; add mussels and steam until they open. Strain broth into another pot, remove mussels from shells, discarding any that are not open, and set aside.

Add saffron and fish stock to broth and cook over medium-low heat until reduced by one third. Stir in corn and cream and simmer until reduced by one third.

Purée mixture in small batches in a blender or food processor, along with the butter. Pour into large serving bowl, and add lobster, mussels, and bell peppers. Season with salt and pepper and serve.

NOTE

• If fish stock is not available, you may wish to purchase some from a local restaurant or substitute unsalted chicken stock.

MARK MONETTE

CREAM OF CARROT SOUP

1 tablespoon canola oil
1 pound carrots, peeled and chopped
½ cup chopped sweet onions
2 cloves garlic
¼ cup brandy

¼ cup Kahlua
5 cups chicken or vegetable stock
2 full tablespoons fresh sage leaves
   (do not chop)
½ cup heavy cream

MAKES: 1 quart
PREPARATION: 20 minutes
COOKING: 1 hour, 20 minutes

PREPARATION

Heat oil in soup pot, add carrots, onions, and garlic and sauté until onions are translucent. Add brandy and Kahlua and simmer 1 minute. Add stock, cover, and simmer 1 hour. Add sage and simmer 3 minutes; remove and discard sage. Purée soup in very small batches, stir in cream, and serve.

NOTE

• Milk may be substituted for heavy cream for those on restricted diets.

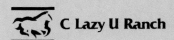

C Lazy U Ranch

C Lazy U Ranch
P.O. Box 379
Granby, Colorado 80446
(970) 887-3344

C Lazy U Ranch, one of the country's outstanding guest ranches, has received both Mobil's five-star and AAA's five-diamond awards for the past thirteen years. Guests dine overlooking a breathtaking expanse of mountains and meadows. Summer or winter, C Lazy U Ranch is an experience of a lifetime.

Cony Creek, Rocky Mountain National Park

STEPHEN REYNOLDS

ASPARAGUS SOUP

2 whole leeks
2 tablespoons olive oil
1 small onion, sliced
3 pounds fresh asparagus
1 ½ quarts chicken stock
2 medium baking potatoes,
　　peeled and roughly chopped
3 garlic cloves
1 tablespoon salt
4 ounces fresh spinach,
　　rinsed and stems removed
Pinch of cayenne pepper
½ cup 2% milk

SERVES: 8
PREPARATION: 10 minutes
COOKING: 1 hour

RENAISSANCE

Renaissance
304 East Hopkins Avenue
Aspen, Colorado 81611
(970) 925-2402

Colorado granite and stucco
walls tempered with French
silk and original art reflect
the life of an American raised
in France. Chef Charles Dale
applies his mastery of classic
French techniques to organically
grown foods, yielding dishes
unique in both style and flavor.

PREPARATION

Remove two thirds of green part from both leeks and slit remaining portion down the side. Rinse to remove dirt or grit and chop roughly. Heat oil in soup kettle, add onions and leeks, and cook over low heat until wilted.

Remove and discard tough ends from asparagus; cut off about 2 inches of the tips and set aside. Place remaining middle sections of asparagus stalks in kettle and cook for 5 minutes. Add chicken stock, potatoes, garlic, and salt. Simmer for 45 minutes. Add half of the reserved asparagus tips and cook an additional 5 minutes. Remove from heat.

In small saucepan, bring 2 cups water to a boil, add remaining asparagus tips, and cook 3 minutes. Remove with slotted spoon and set aside for garnish. In same water, repeat cooking procedure for spinach, then drain and add to soup. Purée soup in small batches in a blender or food processor. Strain and season to taste with salt and cayenne. Return to soup kettle, add milk, and heat thoroughly. Pour into bowls or tureen and garnish with reserved asparagus tips.

NOTES

• This soup can be made in advance through the puréeing step and refrigerated. When ready to serve, add milk and reheat.

• Soup can be served chilled.

CHARLES DALE

CIOPPINO

Roux

2 tablespoons melted butter

2 tablespoons all-purpose flour

Cioppino

4 cherrystone clams, scrubbed

4 greenlip mussels,
scrubbed and beards removed

2 tablespoons butter

1 small onion, medium diced

½ green bell pepper, julienned

⅓ pound button mushrooms, halved

1½ teaspoons kosher salt

2 tablespoons finely chopped
fresh oregano

Pinch of sage

2 tablespoons finely chopped fresh basil

⅛ teaspoon dried thyme

2 teaspoons finely chopped garlic

1½ cups V-8 juice

1 14–ounce can whole pear tomatoes,
with juice

2 tablespoons Worcestershire sauce

½ cup Chablis

1 cup clam juice

½ zucchini, cut in 1 inch wedges

¼ cup black pitted olives, chopped

¼ pound fresh swordfish, cubed

6 jumbo sea scallops

½ pound fresh bay scallops

½ pound small gulf shrimp,
peeled and deveined

4 snow crab claws

SERVES: 4 as an entrée
PREPARATION: 20 minutes
COOKING: 35 minutes

The Briarwood Inn
1630 Eighth Street
Golden, Colorado 80401
(303) 279-3121

*Nestled in the foothills of the
Rockies in the town of Golden,
The Briarwood Inn captures
the essence of European charm.
Enjoy the finest continental
cuisine for lunch, dinner, or
Sunday brunch amidst the
romantic elegance of antiques,
glass etchings, and cozy booths.*

PREPARATION

1. Roux. Melt butter in small saucepan, whisk in flour until smooth and cook for 3–4 minutes. Set aside.

2. Cioppino. Steam clams and mussels until they open, discarding any that do not open. In large saucepan, melt butter and sauté onions, bell peppers, mushrooms, salt, oregano, sage, basil, thyme, and garlic until onions are soft. Add V-8 juice, tomatoes, Worcestershire, wine, and clam juice and bring to a boil. Stir in roux, reduce heat to simmer, and add zucchini, olives, swordfish, scallops, shrimp, crab, clams, and mussels. Bring to boil for 1 minute, then serve immediately.

NOTE

• Garlic bread and a salad make this dish a complete meal.

TOM MORRIS

COOL GRAPE SOUP

Crème fraîche (optional)
1 quart heavy cream
⅔ cup butter, softened

Mint Crema (optional)
1 cup crème fraîche
1 ounce fresh mint, finely chopped

Grape Soup
2½ pounds black grapes
⅓ cup fresh horseradish, peeled and coarsely chopped
Salt and pepper to taste

PREPARATION

1. Crème fraîche. Whisk ingredients together in a bowl. Leave out overnight covered; do not refrigerate.

2. Mint Crema. Whip crème fraîche until it forms soft peaks. Fold in mint.

3. Grape Soup. Wash and dry grapes, then purée with horseradish in small batches. Strain through wire mesh strainer into a bowl, pressing with spatula or spoon to extract as much liquid as possible. Discard skins and season soup with salt and pepper.

4. Serving. Ladle soup into individual bowls and add a dollop of mint crema, if desired.

NOTES

• Crème fraîche can be purchased from many grocery stores. An alternative is simply to garnish each serving with fresh mint leaves.

• This soup is delicious served at room temperature or chilled.

MAKES: 1 quart
PREPARATION: 15 minutes
(crème fraîche is made the day before)

Tante Louise
4900 East Colfax Avenue
Denver, Colorado 80220
(303) 355-4488

Situated in a renovated Victorian bungalow with hardwood floors, candlelit tables, and glowing fireplaces, Tante Louise is a AAA four-diamond restaurant. It features contemporary French-American fare with an impressive selection of more than 350 domestic and imported wines.

MICHAEL DEGENHART

ROASTED TOMATO SOUP

3 pounds tomatoes
2 medium onions, chopped
2 teaspoons minced garlic
3 stalks of celery, chopped
2 medium carrots, chopped
⅓ pound margarine
⅔ cup white wine
10 cups lite chicken stock
1 tablespoon fresh thyme leaves
⅓ cup tightly packed fresh basil leaves
2 teaspoons chopped fresh marjoram leaves
1 teaspoon white pepper

PREPARATION

Preheat oven to 350 degrees. Place tomatoes on cookie sheet and bake for 40 minutes. When cool enough to handle, peel, seed, and chop coarsely.

In a large soup pot, sauté onions, garlic, celery, and carrots in margarine. When soft, add tomatoes and cook for 2–3 minutes. Add wine and stock and simmer until soup begins to thicken, approximately 2 hours. Add thyme, basil, marjoram, and pepper and cook 10 minutes. Serve.

SERVES: 6
PREPARATION: 15 minutes
COOKING: 2 hours, 40 minutes

Palace Arms
The Brown Palace Hotel
321 Seventeenth Street
Denver, Colorado 80202
(303) 297-3111

Denver's only Mobil four-star restaurant, the Palace Arms' elegant atmosphere and contemporary cuisine combine for a memorable dining experience. Stained glass, objets d'art, and antiques dating back to Napoleonic times complement the gracious service and talented culinary staff.

JEFFREY L. ERICKSON

TOMATO THYME SOUP

2 tablespoons olive oil

2 onions, rough cut

2 garlic cloves, minced

2 carrots, peeled and thinly sliced

3 14-ounce cans peeled plum tomatoes

1 bay leaf

1 small bunch fresh thyme,
   leaves picked off stem

Salt and pepper to taste

½ bunch fresh parsley, chopped

½ cup heavy cream, half and half,
   or milk (optional)

PREPARATION

In heavy-bottomed pot, heat olive oil over medium heat. Add onions, garlic, and carrots and cook covered, stirring frequently, until onions are tender and translucent. Add tomatoes, bay leaf, and thyme. Season with salt and pepper and cook until carrots are tender, approximately 20 minutes. Add parsley and cook 5 more minutes. Purée in a blender or food processor; stir in cream or milk, if desired.

SERVES: 6

PREPARATION: 15 minutes

COOKING: 30 minutes

Beano's Cabin
Beaver Creek Resort
P.O. Box 915
Avon, Colorado 81620
(970) 949-9090

Beano's Cabin, situated high above the Beaver Creek resort, is the perfect mountaintop dining experience. Depending on the season, you arrive here via a snowcat-drawn sleigh, horse-drawn wagon, van, or even on horseback. You are then treated to an exceptional six-course prix fixe dinner.

JOSEPH P. KEEGAN

LEEK AND POTATO SOUP

1 ½ tablespoons olive oil

7–8 medium leeks, washed and thinly sliced

Kosher salt to taste

2 pounds potatoes, peeled and cut into bite-sized pieces

12 cups water

¼ cup heavy cream

3 sprigs fresh chervil

White pepper to taste

Croutons as garnish (optional)

PREPARATION

Heat oil in 4–5 quart pot, add leeks, and sauté until softened. Sprinkle with kosher salt, add potatoes and water, and bring to a boil. Reduce heat to medium and cook until potatoes are tender. Reduce heat to low and add cream and chervil. Season with kosher salt and pepper. If you prefer a smooth consistency, purée in a blender. Ladle into individual bowls and garnish with croutons.

NOTE

• Milk may be substituted for the heavy cream.

SERVES: 6
PREPARATION: 10 minutes
COOKING: 25–30 minutes

European Cafe
2460 Arapahoe Avenue
Boulder, Colorado 80302
(303) 938-8250
and
1515 Market Street
Denver, Colorado 80202
(303) 825-6555

Chef Radek Cerny immigrated to the United States from Czechoslovakia. In 1989, a dream was realized with the opening of the European Cafe in Boulder. Here are the best elements of continental ciusine and healthy food are combines in anelegant setting with unrushed service.

RADEK CERNY

Opposite: Along the Dolores River
Overleaf: Chaos Creek, Rocky Mountain National Park

Skewered Ahi Salad
with Roasted Tomato Vinaigrette

Ahi
1 tablespoon chopped fresh basil
1 teaspoon finely chopped garlic
½ cup extra-virgin olive oil
2 teaspoons balsamic vinegar
3 pounds ahi, cut in 1½-inch cubes

Roasted Tomato Vinaigrette
2½ large tomatoes
1½ teaspoons sugar
¾ teaspoon kosher salt
1½ cloves garlic
3 teaspoons balsamic vinegar
½ cup extra-virgin olive oil

Salad
1 red bell pepper, slivered
1 zucchini, julienned
1 yellow squash, halved lengthwise, cut into moons
16 asparagus stalks, blanched
1 pound mixed field greens

SERVES: 8
PREPARATION: 20 minutes
(ahi marinates for 2–4 hours)
COOKING: 8–10 minutes

The Briarwood Inn
1630 Eighth Street
Golden, Colorado 80401
(303) 279-3121

Nestled in the foothills of the Rockies in the town of Golden, The Briarwood Inn captures the essence of European charm. Enjoy the finest continental cuisine unch, dinner, or Sunday brunch amidst the romantic elegance of antiques, glass etchings, and cozy booths.

Preparation

1. Ahi. Combine all ingredients in a nonreactive bowl and marinade for 2–4 hours. Put ahi on skewers and grill or broil until medium-rare.

2. Roasted Tomato Vinaigrette. Cut tomatoes in half and remove seeds using a spoon. Place under broiler or on grill for 3–5 minutes, or until soft, being careful not to blacken. Transfer to blender or food processor, add remaining ingredients, and blend for about 5 minutes. Can be served warm or cold.

3. Serving. Toss salad ingredients with vinaigrette, place on individual plates, and top with ahi. Serve immediately.

Notes
• Ahi is the Hawaiian name for tuna.
• Salmon or swordfish can be substituted for the ahi if it is unavailable. Chicken can also be used.

TOM MORRIS

SEARED SCALLOPS WITH CITRUS COUSCOUS AND SUNDRIED TOMATO VINAIGRETTE

SERVES: 6
PREPARATION: 20 minutes
COOKING: 30 minutes

CACHE
CACHE

Cache Cache
205 South Mill Street
Aspen, Colorado 81611
(970) 925-3835

Cache Cache is an innovative
French Bistro serving the
food of Provençe. In a warm,
cozy atmosphere filled with
fresh flowers and objets d'art,
patrons enjoy healthy foods
prepared without fats
or butter

MICHAEL W. BEARY

Tomato Fondue
2 tomatoes
1 tablespoon olive oil
1 ½ teaspoons finely chopped shallots
¼ cup white wine
Salt and pepper to taste

Couscous
1 orange, zest and fruit
1 lemon, zest and juice
1 cup halved kumquats
½ cup sugar
2 cups couscous

Tomato Vinaigrette
½ cup chopped yellow sundried tomatoes
½ cup tomato fondue
½ cup champagne vinegar
1 cup extra-virgin olive oil
½ teaspoon chopped shallots
½ teaspoon blanched and
    finely chopped garlic
Pinch of salt and pepper

Scallops
1 ½ pounds scallops (depending on size)
2 tablespoons peanut oil
Salt and pepper

Garnish
Enough mixed salad greens
    to circle 6 plates

PREPARATION

1. Tomato Fondue. Bring large pot of water to a boil. Meanwhile, cut an X on base of both tomatoes and remove stem core. Gently add tomatoes to boiling water and when skins begin to separate, remove tomatoes from pot. Run under cold water and pull off skins. To extract seeds, hold tomatoes in palm of hand and squeeze gently. Chop pulp and mix with remaining ingredients in small saucepan. Cook over medium-low heat until very soft, approximately 15 minutes.

2. Couscous. Purée all ingredients, except couscous, in a blender or food processor. Add enough water to mixture so volume equals 4 cups. Transfer to saucepan, bring to boil, and stir in couscous. Remove from heat, cover tightly, and let stand 15 minutes. Remove cover and stir with fork until couscous is fluffed.

3. Tomato Vinaigrette. Place all ingredients in blender or food processor and purée.

4. Scallops. Mix scallops, peanut oil, and salt and pepper. Heat large pan over high heat and sear scallops until medium rare; center will be translucent.

5. Serving. Mound a serving of couscous in center of each plate. Arrange salad greens around couscous and place scallops on and around couscous; drizzle with vinaigrette.

PAPAYA MARINATED LOIN OF LAMB WITH CARAMELIZED GINGER VINAIGRETTE, MATSUTAKE MUSHROOMS AND SPRING GREENS

Papaya Marinade

1 very ripe papaya, peeled and seeded

1 lemon, juice only

½ cup olive oil

Lamb

4 6-ounce lamb loins

Black pepper

Caramelized Ginger Vinaigrette

¼ cup sugar

3 tablespoons peeled and
  diced gingerroot

¼ cup water

3 lemons, juice only

1 cup rice vinegar

1 cup olive oil

Mushrooms

8 large matsutake mushrooms

4 tablespoons soy sauce

Salad

8 cups spring greens, washed

2 grapefruits, sectioned

2 packages daikon sprouts

2 Belgian endives

SERVES: 8

PREPARATION: 30 minutes
(lamb marinates 24 hours)

COOKING: 25 minutes

Cliff Young's

Cliff Young's
700 East 17th Avenue
Denver, Colorado 80203
(303) 831-8900

*Cliff Young's is Denver's answer
to elegant fine dining. With
the romantic, richly decorated
Amethyst Room, the stately
Crystal Room, or the nonpareil
main dining room, Cliff Young's
is a truly wonderful epicurean
experience.*

PREPARATION

1. Marinade and Lamb. Purée all marinade ingredients in blender or food processor. Trim lamb of silver skin and fat and sprinkle with pepper. Place lamb in a nonreactive bowl, cover with marinade, and refrigerate for 24 hours, turning over occasionally. At the time of serving, remove from marinade and grill to personal preference.

2. Caramelized Ginger Vinaigrette. Combine sugar, gingerroot, water, and lemon juice in small pan. Cook over medium heat until caramel forms on gingerroot. Transfer to blender, add vinegar, and purée. Slowly drizzle in oil until mixture forms a homogenous liquid. Strain and reserve liquid.

3. Mushrooms. Remove and discard stems from mushrooms. Clean, brush with soy sauce, and grill for 2 minutes per side.

4. Serving. Toss greens, grapefruit sections, daikon sprouts, and endive with vinaigrette, and place in center of each plate. Slice lamb, arrange over greens, and top with mushrooms. Drizzle with a little vinaigrette and serve.

NOTE

• Matsutake mushrooms and daikon sprouts can be found in Oriental markets and health food stores. Shiitake mushrooms and spicy alfalfa sprouts can be substituted.

SEAN BRASEL

Avocado, Grapefruit and Arugula Salad

4 ripe avocados, sliced
1½ grapefruits, sectioned
4 handfuls of arugula, cleaned
2 tablespoons extra-virgin olive oil
2 tablespoons juice from fresh grapefruit
Freshly ground black pepper

SERVES: 4
PREPARATION: 5 minutes

PREPARATION

Toss avocado, grapefruit section, and arugula with oil and grapefruit juice. Season with pepper to taste and serve on cold plates.

The Wildflower
The Lodge at Vail
174 East Gore Creek Drive
Vail, Colorado 81657
(970) 476-5011
(800) 331-LODG

Creative American cuisine and terraced views of Vail Mountain combine for spectacular gourmet dining in timeless elegance at The Wildflower. Chef Jim Cohen's innovative fare has received national recognition from the Mobil Travel Guide, AAA, the James Beard Foundation, and Travel/Holiday magazine.

JAMES E. COHEN

Longs Peak, Rocky Mountain National Park

Kit Carson Salad
with Chipolte Dressing

Chicken

Pinch of pepper

⅛ teaspoon minced fresh oregano

⅛ teaspoon fresh parsley

⅛ teaspoon minced fresh thyme

⅛ teaspoon lemon zest

1 cup white wine

2 cups unsalted chicken broth

1 small onion, sliced

1 stalk celery, sliced

4 boneless, skinless chicken breast halves

Salad

4 cups mixed greens

1⅓ cups canned garbanzo beans, drained

1 avocado, sliced

2 tomatoes, each sliced into 6 wedges

12 slices cucumber

½ cup diced jicama

¼ cup grated Monterey Jack cheese

4 hard-boiled eggs, sliced

1 red bell pepper, julienned

1 Belgian endive

Chipolte Dressing

1 egg yolk

½ garlic clove

½ lime, juice only

¾ cup canola oil

¼ cup olive oil

¼ of 1 canned chipolte chili

2 tablespoons honey

Salt and pepper to taste

SERVES: 4 as an entrée
PREPARATION: 20 minutes
COOKING: 20 minutes

The Fort

The Fort
19192 Route 8
Morrison, Colorado 80465
(303) 697-4771

This unique restaurant, patterned after one of Colorado's first settlement forts, offers the finest in food and drink of the early West. Nestled in the foothills with spectacular views of Denver, The Fort specializes in the unusual, from rattlesnake cocktails to wild Montana huckleberry sundaes.

PREPARATION

1. Chicken. Make a spice bag containing pepper, oregano, parsley, thyme, and lemon zest. Place bag in large saucepan along with wine, chicken broth, onions, and celery. Bring to a boil, reduce heat to a simmer, add chicken breasts, and poach until cooked. Remove breasts and refrigerate to chill.

2. Chipolte Dressing. Place all ingredients in blender or food processor and blend until smooth.

3. Salad. Divide all ingredients into 4 equal portions. Place greens in 4 large bowls and decorate each salad with remaining ingredients, arranging 3 endive leaves, straight up, along rim of each salad.

4. Serving. Slice each chicken breast into strips, place in center of each salad, and drizzle with chipolte dressing.

NOTES

- The chicken can be grilled or broiled instead of poached.
- Substitute or add your favorite vegetables to salad.

Michael R. Barnett
MICHAEL R. BARNETT

SERVES: 2 as an entrée, 4 as a salad
PREPARATION: 10 minutes
COOKING: 10 minutes

L'apogée
911 Lincoln Avenue
Steamboat Springs, Colorado
80477
(970) 879-1919

Stained glass, objets d'art, and
fresh flowers create an intimate,
romantic atmoshpere at L'apogée.
French cuisine with an Asian flare,
an exceptional, award-winning wine
list, and superb service transport Old
World elegance to Steamboat Springs.

SUMMER SIZZLIN' SEAFOOD SALAD

½ cup penne pasta
6 ounces small to medium shrimp,
    peeled and deveined
6 ounces bay scallops
All-purpose flour
2 tablespoons olive oil
2 teaspoons chopped garlic
1 teaspoon sambal paste or
    crushed red chilies *(see Notes)*
1 tablespoon balsamic vinegar
2 tablespoons white wine
¼ cup unsalted chicken broth
2 tablespoons butter
Salt and pepper to taste
1 tablespoon chopped fresh parsley,
    thyme, basil, or oregano
2 large handfuls mixed greens

PREPARATION

Cook penne pasta according to package directions. Meanwhile, lightly dust shrimp and scallops with flour. Heat oil in medium skillet, add shrimp and scallops, and sauté until lightly browned. Stir in garlic, sambal, vinegar, white wine, and chicken broth and bring to boil. Reduce heat and add butter, a bit at a time. Season with salt, pepper, and herbs of choice. Combine with drained pasta. Toss salad greens and seafood-pasta mixture in large bowl. Serve.

NOTES

• Butter maybe omitted entirely or substituted with margarine.

• Sambal is an Indonesian red chili paste. It can be found in Oriental markets and health food stores. The most common brand is Sambal Oeleck.

RICHARD BILLINGHAM

WARM FARMER'S SALAD

3 tablespoons olive oil
2 cloves garlic, minced
4 ounces crumbled Gorgonzola cheese
¼ pound arugula
1 head romaine lettuce
¼ pound radicchio
3 cups sourdough croutons
Salt and pepper to taste

PREPARATION

In a large sauté pan, heat oil, add garlic and Gorgonzola, and sauté until cheese begins to melt. Add salad greens and croutons and cook until greens begin to wilt. Season with salt and pepper.

SERVES: 8
PREPARATION: 5 minutes
COOKING: 5 minutes

TUSCANY

Tuscany
Loews Giorgio Hotel
4150 East Mississippi Avenue
Denver, Colorado 80222
(303) 782-9300

With fresh-cut flowers, marble fireplace, and an evening harpist, the Tuscany is the perfect setting for dining on exquisitely prepared Italian cuisine. The award-winning menu is complemented by a large selection of Italian wines. Tuscany is ideal for celebrating any occasion— or creating one.

TIM A. FIELDS

SALAD GREENS WITH
SWEET TOASTED SESAME DRESSING

¼ cup sesame seeds

½ cup rice vinegar

2 tablespoons honey

1 teaspoon salt

¼ teaspoon white pepper

¼ teaspoon dry mustard

1 ½ cups soybean salad oil

Enough firm salad greens,
    such as romaine, to cover 8 plates

SERVES: 6

PREPARATION: 10 minutes

PREPARATION

Toast sesame seeds in sauté pan on low heat, tossing and stirring frequently, until golden brown. Remove from heat and set aside. In food processor, combine vinegar, honey, salt, pepper, and mustard. While processor is running, add oil, pouring very slowly. Add sesame seeds and process for 10 seconds. Divide greens among 8 plates and drizzle with dressing.

Le Bosquet
201 Elk Avenue
Crested Butte, Colorado 81224
(970) 349-5808

Located 9,000 feet above sea level in the heart of the Colorado Rockies, Le Bosquet serves exquisite French cuisine. Its wine list has received The Wine Spectator's *award of excellence. Escape from the everyday world to relax and enjoy good conversation, food, and wine at Le Bosquet.*

VICTOR R. SHEPARD

WILD HERB SALAD WITH PICKLED BEETS

Rosemary Oil
1 sprig fresh rosemary
¼ cup olive oil

Toasted Pine Nut and Apple Dressing
¼ cup pine nuts
½ tablespoon brown sugar
1 teaspoon lime juice
3 tablespoons apple juice
5 tablespoons apple cider vinegar
1 tablespoon toasted poppy seeds
Salt and pepper to taste
¼ cup canola oil
½ cup olive oil
2 tablespoons chopped fresh chervil

Pickled Baby Beets
¾ cup water
¼ cup wine
½ cup vinegar
¼ cup pickling spice
½ cup sugar
¼ cup salt
40 baby beets

Wild Herbs
2 pounds wild herbs
    (arugula, red giant, basil, sorrel,
    minzuna, etc.)
1 cup pine nuts, toasted

SERVES: 4
PREPARATION: 45 minutes
(oil sits 24 hours)
COOKING: 15 minutes

NORMANDY
restaurant français

Normandy
1515 Madison Street
Denver, Colorado 80206
(303) 321-3311

*Walking into the Normandy
is entering a world of simple
elegance. Antique leaded-glass
windows and period furniture
make this restored turn-of-the-
century home the perfect location
for Chef Robert Mancuso,
a member of Culinary Team
USA, to create award-winning
French dishes.*

ROBERT MANCUSO

PREPARATION

1. Rosemary Oil. Place rosemary in jar, add olive oil, and place in a location where it will receive long sun exposure and stay warm for 24 hours. Strain before using.

2. Toasted Pine Nut and Apple Dressing. Heat pine nuts in sauté pan until toasted, then grind in blender or food processor and set aside. In same saucepan, heat brown sugar and lime juice until caramelized. Stir in apple juice, then set aside to cool. When cool, add remaining ingredients, except oils and chervil, and blend well. Slowly whisk in oils, then add chervil.

3. Pickled Beets. Combine all ingredients, except beets, in large saucepan. Bring to a boil, add beets, and boil for 2–3 minutes.

4. Serving. In small sauté pan, heat 1 cup pine nuts until toasted. Toss wild herbs with dressing and mound in middle of cold plates. Arrange beets around herbs, drizzle with rosemary oil, and sprinkle with toasted pine nuts.

Opposite: Wildflowers, San Juan Mountains
Overleaf: Marsh marigolds, Raggeds Wilderness

AHI AU POIVRE WITH
LEMON-TARRAGON-WHITE WINE SAUCE

Lemon-Tarragon-White Wine Sauce
½ cup white wine
1 tablespoon chopped shallots
1 tablespoon chopped fresh tarragon,
    or 1 teaspoon dried
½ cup heavy whipping cream
¾ pound unsalted butter
1 lemon, juice only
Kosher salt
Black pepper to taste
Dash of Tabasco

Ahi au Poivre
4 7-ounce, 1½-inch thick ahi steaks *(see Note)*
Coarsely ground pepper
Oil for sautéing

Garnish
Chopped fresh tarragon
4 nasturtium blossoms (optional)

SERVES: 4
PREPARATION: 20 minutes
COOKING: 10 minutes

Soupçon
127 A Elk Avenue
Crested Butte, Colorado 81224
(970) 349-5448

Soupçon offers a warm country atmosphere in an intimate setting—there are only nine tables in this gem of the Rockies. Chef-owner Mac Bailey's mission is to "use the freshest ingredients, start from scratch, and make good food."

PREPARATION

1. Lemon-Tarragon-White Wine Sauce. In medium saucepan, mix wine, shallots, and tarragon and bring to a boil. Reduce heat and simmer until liquid is reduced by half. Stir in cream and reduce again by half. Add butter in chunks, whisking over low heat until butter is absorbed and sauce thickens.

Add lemon juice, salt, pepper, and Tabasco and reduce slightly. Adjust seasonings to taste: sauce should be fairly intense and tart. Strain and keep warm. (If done properly, the sauce should look creamy—not oily.)

2. Ahi au Poivre. Heavily coat both sides of fish with fresh coarsely ground pepper. Heat oil in large sauté pan over high heat, add fish, and sauté briefly (3–4 minutes per side) until medium-rare, or to personal preference.

3. Serving. Coat plates with sauce, place ahi on plate, sprinkle with chopped fresh tarragon, and, if desired, garnish with a nasturtium blossom.

NOTE

• Ahi is the Hawaiian name for tuna.

MAC BAILEY

CRAB SOUFFLÉ

SERVES: 6
PREPARATION: 15 minutes
COOKING: 20–25 minutes

4½ tablespoons unsalted butter

Grated Parmesan cheese,
    enough to dust soufflé dishes

3½ tablespoons all-purpose flour

1½ cups milk

⅓ cup white wine

6 egg yolks

1 tablespoon Dijon mustard

1 cup flaked crabmeat

1 cup grated Swiss cheese

½ teaspoon each minced fresh
    chervil, tarragon, and chives

Salt and pepper to taste

Pinch of nutmeg

12 egg whites

Pinch of cream of tartar

12 crab claws and
    6 tablespoons clarified butter
    as garnish (optional)

Tall Timber

Tall Timber
Box 90
Silverton Star Route
Durango, Colorado 81301
(970) 259-4813

Tall Timber, located in a wilderness setting in the heart of the San Juan Mountains, pampers its guests with five-star and five-diamond service. No roads lead to this luxury retreat; all guests arrive by either narrow-gauge railroad or helicopter to enjoy international cuisine and a variety of indoor and outdoor activities.

PREPARATION

Preheat oven to 375 degrees. Butter inside of 6 individual soufflé dishes with 1 tablespoon of the butter. Sprinkle lightly with Parmesan cheese. Melt remaining 3½ tablespoons of butter in saucepan, stir in flour, and cook 3–4 minutes. Whisk in milk and wine and cook, stirring constantly, until thick. Remove from heat. Add egg yolks, 1 at a time, mixing well after each addition. Stir in remaining ingredients, except egg whites and cream of tartar, and set aside. The recipe can be made ahead to this point and refrigerated. Bring to room temperature before continuing.

Beat egg whites, adding cream of tartar, until stiff peaks form. Gently fold into milk-and-egg-yolk mixture. Pour into prepared dishes and bake for approximately 20–25 minutes. Center should be slightly runny, edges firm.

As an optional garnish, steam crab claws and garnish each serving with 2 claws and a small ramekin of clarified butter.

DENNIS J. SHAKAN

FRESHWATER STRIPED BASS WITH FENNEL-TOMATO MARMALADE

Marinade
¼ cup chopped fennel tops
¼ clip olive oil
4 garlic cloves; finely chopped
¼ teaspoon white pepper

Striped Bass
8 5- to 6-ounce striped bass fillets
1 tablespoon kosher salt

Fennel-Tomato Marmalade
1 white onion, finely diced
2 garlic cloves, finely chopped
8 Roma tomatoes
    peeled, seeded, and diced;
    reserving 2 tablespoons for sauce
1 tablespoon chopped fresh thyme
Salt and pepper to taste
¼ cup olive oil
5 star anise pods
2 red onions, sliced lengthwise
6 fennel bulbs, cored and sliced
¼ cup Pernod

Sauce Vierge
¼ cup extra-virgin olive oil
I tablespoon each chopped fresh parsley,
    chervil, and tarragon
2 tablespoons chopped tomatoes
1 lemon, juice only

Garnish
8 sprigs fennel tops

SERVES: 8
PREPARATION: 30 minutes
COOKING: 1 hour, 10 minutes

RENAISSANCE

Renaissance
304 East Hopkins Avenue
Aspen, Colorado 81611
(970) 925-2402

Colorado granite and stucco walls tempered with French silk and original art reflect the life of an American raised in France. Chef Charles Dale applies his mastery of classic French techniques to organically grown foods, yielding dishes unique in both style and flavor.

PREPARATION

1. *Marinade.* Mix all ingredients in small bowl. Spread marinade liberally over flesh side of each fish fillet. Cover fish with plastic wrap and refrigerate until ready to use.

2. *Fennel-Tomato Marmalade.* In small saucepan, sauté white onions in small amount of oil until translucent. Add garlic and tomatoes, cook 20 minutes, add thyme, cook another 5 minutes, then season with salt and pepper.

In large sauté pan, heat ¼ cup oil, add star anise, and cook for 2 minutes, stirring continuously. Add red onions, cook 1 minute, then stir in fennel. Reduce heat to medium-low and cook 20 minutes, adding water as necessary to prevent sticking or burning. Add tomato mixture and Pernod and simmer for 20 minutes.

3. *Sauce Vierge.* Gently mix all ingredients in small bowl.

4. *Striped Bass.* Preheat oven to 350 degrees. Sprinkle fish with kosher salt. Sauté fish in olive oil for 1 minute on both sides, flesh side first. (The fish can be refrigerated at this point for at least 1 hour, but bring to room temperature before baking.) Bake for 4–5 minutes.

5. *Serving.* Spoon hot marmalade onto each plate and top with fish and 1 teaspoon sauce. Sprinkle with fresh lemon juice, garnish with sprig of fennel on side of each plate, and serve immediately.

CHARLES DALE

NOTE

• Halibut, black sea bass, or brook trout also may be used in this recipe.

GRILLED SWORDFISH A LA THAI

Swordfish
4 6–ounce swordfish steaks
1–2 tablespoons olive oil

Thai Sauce
¼ cup soy sauce
¼ cup fresh lime or lemon juice
¼ cup extra-virgin olive oil

Garnish
¼ cup chopped fresh chives

SERVES: 4
PREPARATION: 5 minutes
COOKING: 10–12 minutes

PREPARATION

1. Swordfish. Lightly brush swordfish with oil and grill or broil until fish is slightly translucent in center, approximately 10 minutes.

2. Thai Sauce. Combine soy sauce, lemon or lime juice, and olive oil in small bowl.

3. Serving. Place fish on individual plates, spoon on some sauce, and top with chives.

NOTES

• If you like ginger, top the fish with grated gingerroot.
• This recipe works well with any broiled fish.

The Left Bank

The Left Bank
83 Gore Creek Drive
Vail, Colorado 81657
(970) 476-3696

Born and raised in France, Chef Luc Meyer opened The Left Bank in 1970 and for twenty-five years the restaurant has enjoyed an international reputation. People from around the world return here often for outstanding French cuisine served in a cozy, elegant atmosphere.

LUC MEYER
Recipe reprinted with permission
from author Luc Meyer

Aspen grove, Routt National Forest

SHRIMP AND SCALLOPS IN LEMON GRASS AND THYME BROTH WITH VEGETABLE ROOT RAVIOLI

Vegetable Root Ravioli

½ carrot, peeled and diced

¼ celery root, peeled and diced

1 small zucchini, diced

1 turnip, peeled and diced

1 parsnip, peeled and diced

½ onion, diced

1 thumb-sized gingerroot, peeled and diced

½ cup heavy cream

Salt and pepper to taste

1 egg, beaten

1 package wonton wrappers

Broth

4 cups chicken broth

1 thumb-sized gingerroot, peeled and sliced

1 blade lemon grass, finely sliced

¼ teaspoon whole cardamom

1 teaspoon minced fresh thyme leaves

2 tablespoons virgin olive oil

2 tablespoons soy sauce

Vegetable Garnish

3 zucchini, julienned

3 carrots, julienned

2 teaspoons olive oil

½ teaspoon, minced fresh thyme leaves

Salt and pepper to taste

Shrimp and Scallops

30 sea scallops

2–4 tablespoons olive oil

30 shrimp, peeled and deveined

SERVES: 6

PREPARATION: 30 minutes

COOKING: 40 minutes

Picasso

The Lodge at Cordillera

2205 Cordillera Way

Edwards, Colorado 81632

(970) 926-2200

Located on top of a mountain with spectacular views of New York Mountain and the Vail Valley, Picasso's is European elegance with Rocky Mountain scenery.. Its award-winning contemporary French cuisine and outstanding wine list make any occasion here special.

PREPARATION

1. Vegetable Root Ravioli. Preheat oven to 350 degrees. Combine vegetables, gingerroot, cream, and salt and pepper in baking dish and bake until vegetables are soft. Remove from oven and cool. Put 1 tablespoon of cooled vegetable mixture in center of wonton wrapper, brush edges of wrapper with egg, and place another wonton wrapper on top of mixture. Press out excess air, lightly pinch edges, and cut with round cookie cutter or leave square. Makes 36 ravioli.

2. Broth. Mix all ingredients in medium saucepan. Bring to a boil, reduce heat, cover, and simmer for 30 minutes.

3. Vegetable Garnish. Sauté vegetables in oil until carrots begin to soften. Stir in thyme and salt and pepper. Keep warm.

4. Shrimp and Scallops. Sear scallops quickly in oil until golden. In separate pan sear shrimp until pink. Drain on paper towels to absorb excess oil.

5. Serving. Poach ravioli in broth until tender but still firm. In large soup plate, place julienned vegetables, ravioli, shrimp, and scallops. Ladle in broth.

FABRICE BEAUDOIN

HALIBUT WITH RED BEET SAUCE
AND FRESH PEACH AND CHERRY SALSA

SERVES: 4
PREPARATION: 15 minutes
COOKING: 1 hour

European Cafe
2460 Arapahoe Avenue
Boulder, Colorado 80302
(303) 938-8250
and
1515 Market Street
Denver, Colorado 80202
(303) 825-6555

*Chef Radek Cerny immigrated
to the United States from
Czechoslovakia. In 1989, a
dream was realized with the
opening of the European Cafe
in Boulder. Here the best
elements of continental cuisine
and healthy food are combined
in an elegant setting with
unrushed service.*

RADEK CERNY

Peach and Cherry Salsa
2 ripe peaches, peeled, pitted, and chopped
1 cup cherries, quartered
⅓ cup chopped red onions
⅔ cup sweet corn, cut off cob
1 tablespoon chopped fresh cilantro
1 lime, juice only
2 tablespoons olive oil
Salt and pepper to taste

Beet Sauce
2 medium beets, scrubbed
¼ cup white wine
1 tablespoon chopped shallots
Heavy cream or milk (optional)

Halibut
Olive oil for sautéing
4 5- to 6-ounce halibut fillets
1 lemon, juice only

PREPARATION

1. Peach and Cherry Salsa. Combine all ingredients in glass bowl
and chill for 1 hour.

2. Beet Sauce. Wrap beets in foil and bake in 350-degree oven until soft,
about 1 hour. (Or place beets in covered glass container and cook in microwave oven
until done.) Transfer to blender or food processor, add wine and shallots, and purée
until smooth. If desired, add splash of cream or milk. Keep warm.

3. Halibut. Heat oil in a large sauté pan, add halibut and a splash of
lemon juice, and cook until fish is springy to the touch and slightly translucent in center.

4. Serving. Spoon beet sauce in a half-moon shape onto each plate, place
halibut above sauce, and top with peach and cherry salsa.

NOTES
• Any firm white fish, such as swordfish, can be substituted.
• The fish can also be grilled, but use a fish steak instead of fillet.
• The salsa is also good with grilled pork and chicken.

MAHI MAHI AU POIVRE WITH POTATO RISOTTO AND CREAMY MIXED PEPPERCORN SAUCE

Potato Risotto

2 cups chicken stock

2 tablespoons white wine

2 medium potatoes,
    peeled into diced ¼-inch pieces

½ teaspoon chopped garlic

2 tablespoons butter

⅓ cup freshly grated Parmesan cheese

Salt to taste

Mahi Mahi

1 tablespoon olive oil

Pinch of salt

2 6-ounce Mahi Mahi steaks

1 tablespoon coarsely ground
    black pepper

Creamy Mixed Peppercorn Sauce

2 tablespoons brandy

1 cup heavy cream

2 tablespoons veal or beef stock

½ teaspoon pink peppercorns

½ teaspoon green peppercorns

4 tablespoons butter, cut into pieces

Salt to taste

SERVES: 2

PREPARATION: 15 minutes

COOKING: 35 minutes

Zenith American Grill
1735 Arapahoe Street
Denver, Colorado 80202
(303) 820-2800

*Zenith American Grill is
home to a new class of western
cooking. Chef Kevin Taylor
uses regional ingredients and
organic vegetables when
creating dishes with Asian,
Italian, or Southwestern
influences. Each plate is a
piece of art, presented like
a de Kooning canvas.*

PREPARATION

1. Potato Risotto. In medium saucepan, boil chicken stock, wine, potatoes, and garlic until almost all liquid is gone. Stir in butter, Parmesan cheese, and salt.

2. Mahi Mahi. Preheat oven to 350 degrees. In ovenproof sauté pan, heat oil over medium-high heat. Add salt, sprinkle fish with ground pepper, and sauté on one side only for about 4 minutes. Turn over and place in oven, and bake for 4–6 minutes, depending on thickness. Fish should be springy to the touch and slightly translucent in center. Remove fish from pan but keep warm.

3. Creamy Mixed Peppercorn Sauce. In pan used for fish, add brandy and touch a match to side of pan (be very careful, for flames can be high). Once flame extinguishes, add cream, stock, and pink and green peppercorns, and boil until liquid is reduced by two thirds. Remove from heat and whisk in butter 1 piece at a time, until fully incorporated. Season with salt.

4. Serving. Place risotto on hot plate, top with fish, then spoon on sauce.

NOTE

• Steamed vegetables are a wonderful accompaniment to this entrée.

KEVIN TAYLOR

New Zealand Orange Roughy Polynesian Style

SERVES: 4
PREPARATION: 10 minutes
COOKING: 8–10 minutes

La Renaissance

La Renaissance
217 East Routt Avenue
Pueblo, Colorado 81004
(719) 543-6367

La Renaissance typifies casual, relaxed dining in a unique atmosphere. Located in a lovely old church built in 1888 with high, vaulted ceilings and stained-glass windows, La Renaissance offers seasonal delicacies combined with traditional cuisine to produce an exceptional dining experience.

Orange Roughy
4 6- to 8-ounce orange roughy fillets
All-purpose flour
2 eggs
1 tablespoon milk
1–1¼ cups shredded coconut

Sauce
1 pound butter
1 teaspoon lemon juice
1½ teaspoons beef stock

PREPARATION

1. Orange Roughy. Pat fillets dry and dust with flour. In shallow bowl, whisk eggs and milk. When smooth, add enough coconut so mixture is thick. Dip fillets in mixture and broil until golden brown on both sides, turning only once.

2. Sauce. Melt butter and whisk in lemon juice and beef stock.

3. Serving. Place fillets on each plate and drizzle with sauce.

NOTE

• This dish is very rich. For those on a restricted diet, pat fillets dry, sprinkle lightly with white pepper, and broil until golden brown. Serve with lemon or orange wedges. Another serving option is to top fillets with chopped fresh pineapple and a sprinkling of coconut, about ½ teaspoon per fillet.

ROBERT A. FREDREGILL

STRAUD FREDREGILL

SALMON WITH GINGER GLAZE

Ginger Glaze
3 cups clam juice
½ cup soy sauce
6 tablespoons orange marmalade
1 tablespoon minced garlic
¼ teaspoon cayenne pepper
¼ cup molasses
4 tablespoons sugar
¼ cup lemon juice
5 tablespoons peeled, grated gingerroot
2 tablespoons arrowroot
¼ cup cooking sherry
¾ pound unsalted butter

Salmon
8 6-ounce salmon steaks

PREPARATION

1. Ginger Glaze. In a medium saucepan, boil clam juice and cook until liquid is reduced by half. Whisk in soy sauce, marmalade, garlic, cayenne, molasses, sugar, lemon juice, and gingerroot. Simmer covered over medium-low heat for 10 minutes. In small bowl, combine arrowroot and sherry, stirring until smooth. Whisk into marmalade mixture and remove from heat. Cut butter into pieces and whisk into mixture, 1 piece at a time.

2. Salmon. Preheat oven to 400 degrees. Bake salmon on greased baking sheet for 5–7 minutes or until fish is springy to the touch and the center is slightly translucent.

3. Serving. Place salmon on individual plates. Spoon 1 tablespoon ginger glaze over each steak and serve immediately.

NOTE

• For those on restricted diets, margarine may be substituted for butter in the ginger glaze or use neither butter or margarine, which results in a stronger flavored sauce.

SERVES: 8
PREPARATION: 10 minutes
COOKING: 20 minutes

Le Bosquet
201 Elk Avenue
Crested Butte, Colorado 81224
(970) 349-5808

Located 9,000 feet above sea level in the heart of the Colorado Rockies, Le Bosquet serves exquisite French cuisine. Its wine list has received The Wine Spectator's *award of excellence. Escape from the everyday world to relax and enjoy good conversation, food, and wine at Le Bosquet.*

VICTOR R. SHEPARD

SALMON IN A BEET SAUCE

SERVES: 6
PREPARATION: 5 minutes
COOKING: 20 minutes

The Savoy
535 Third Street
Berthoud, Colorado 80513
(970) 532-4095

*From the moment you enter
The Savoy you are immersed in
a French-country atmosphere.
Owner Chantal Martini serves
Contential-French cuisine
expertly prepared and presented
by Chef Jean Martini. The
Savoy is the perfect spot to
celebrate any occasion.*

Beet Sauce
1 tablespoon cornstarch
2 tablespoons water
1 tablespoon olive oil
1 shallot, chopped
½ cup clam juice *(see Notes)*
Pinch of salt and pepper
1 cup beet juice *(see Notes)*
¼ cup heavy cream (optional)

Salmon
6 6-ounce salmon fillets
3–4 cups water *(see Notes)*

PREPARATION

1. Beet Sauce. In small bowl, dissolve cornstarch in water. In medium saucepan, heat oil, add shallots, and sauté until translucent. Add clam juice and reduce by half. Stir in salt, pepper, and beet juice and bring to a boil. Remove from heat, add cornstarch mixture, stirring continuously, and, if desired, finish with cream.

2. Salmon. Bring water to a boil, add salmon, and poach until fish is springy to the touch and translucent in center.

NOTES

• Clam juice and beet juice can be purchased in health food stores and some grocery stores.

• When poaching fish, the water level should cover the fish steak.

JEAN MARTINI

SALMON WITH TOMATO AND CHIVES

5 5-ounce salmon fillets
Coarse sea salt
Black pepper
8 tomatoes, peeled, seeded, and diced
¼ cups chopped chives
1 tablespoon roughly chopped fresh parsley
3 tablespoons balsamic vinegar
1 tablespoon extra-virgin olive oil

PREPARATION

Heat nonstick pan over medium heat, season salmon with sea salt and pepper, and place fillets in pan, skin side down. Cook slowly until top of fish is the only portion that looks raw (until it just begins to turn color). The bottom will be very crisp. Add tomatoes and cook until warm. Stir in chives, parsley, and then vinegar. Place salmon on platter or individual plates, top with tomato mixture and drizzle with oil.

NOTE

• This dish can be served with roasted new potatoes rolled in coarse sea salt.

SERVES: 4
PREPARATION: 5 minutes
COOKING: 10 minutes

The Wildflower
The Lodge at Vail
174 East Gore Creek Drive
Vail, Colorado 81657
(970) 476-5011
(800) 331-LODG

Creative American cuisine and terraced views of Vail Mountain combine for spectacular gourmet dining in timeless elegance at The Wildflower. Chef Jim Cohen's innovative fare has received national recognition from Mobil Travel Guide, *AAA, the James Beard Foundation, and* Travel/Holiday *magazine.*

JAMES E. COHEN

Pawnee Buttes, Pawnee National Grasslands

PAN-SEARED SCALLOPS WITH
BALSAMIC VINEGAR GLAZE AND TOMATO-CAPER RELISH

SERVES: 4
PREPARATION: 25 minutes
COOKING: 35 minutes

Normandy
1515 Madison Street
Denver, Colorado 80206
(303) 321-3311

Walking into the Normandy is entering a world of simple elegance. Antique leaded-glass windows and period furniture make this restored turn-of-the-century home the perfect location for Chef Robert Mancuso, a member of Culinary Team USA, to create award-winning French dishes.

ROBERT MANCUSO

Tomato-Caper Relish
Olive oil
1 tablespoon minced garlic
1 tablespoon minced shallots
¼ cup white wine
6 tomatoes, peeled, seeded, and finely chopped
¼ cup capers, drained

Cilantro-Peanut Sauce
1 tablespoon olive oil
2 tablespoons minced gingerroot
1 onion, diced
1 tablespoon ground coriander
1 teaspoon black pepper
1 teaspoon minced fresh thyme leaves
1 bay leaf
2 cups water
1 bunch fresh cilantro, stems removed
½ cup peanuts

Crisp Potato Cakes
1 pound potatoes, peeled and shredded
2 tablespoons lemon juice
1 egg
¼ cup all-purpose flour

Scallops
Olive oil
1½ pounds large scallops
¼ cup balsamic vinegar

PREPARATION

1. Tomato-Caper Relish. Heat small amount of oil in saucepan and sauté garlic and shallots until tender. Add wine and stir, scraping up any garlic and shallots stuck to bottom of pan. Add tomatoes and capers and stew gently, uncovered, for 20 minutes.

2. Cilantro-Peanut Sauce. Heat oil in medium sauté pan and sauté gingerroot and onions until translucent. Add coriander, pepper, thyme, and bay leaf, and increase heat, cooking until onions begin to caramelize. Add water, simmer for 2 minutes, and remove from heat. Purée in blender or food processor with cilantro and peanuts, then chill.

3. Crisp Potato Cakes. Combine all ingredients and form into very thin cakes. Sauté until golden brown in Teflon pan or skillet coated with cooking spray.

4. Scallops. Heat small amount of oil in large skillet and sauté scallops until golden brown. Add vinegar and cook until liquid is evaporated, stirring often.

5. Serving. Ladle sauce onto each plate, spoon relish in center, encircle with scallops, and place potato cake to one side.

Sesame Seed-Crusted Bass with Fried Spinach and Cilantro-Lime Vinaigrette

Grapefruit Compote
½ cup port wine
1½ cups red wine vinegar
½ cup sugar
3 grapefruits

Cilantro-Lime Vinaigrette
¼ cup lime juice
½ cup cider vinegar
½ cup rice vinegar
½ cup olive oil
Pinch each of nutmeg, ground cloves,
   and ground cinnamon
¼ teaspoon minced fresh cilantro
¼ cup honey

Fried Spinach
Oil for frying
12 ounces spinach, stemmed

Sesame Seed-Crusted Bass
¾ cup black sesame seeds
¾ cup white sesame seeds
3 tablespoons ground ginger
4 6-ounce bass fillets, boned and skinned

SERVES: 4
PREPARATION: 30 minutes
COOKING: 30 minutes

Palace Arms
The Brown Palace Hotel
321 Seventeenth Street
Denver, Colorado 80202
(303) 297-3111

Denver's only Mobil four-star restaurant, the Palace Arms' elegant atmosphere and contemporary cuisine combine for a memorable dining experience. Stained glass, objets d'art, and antiques dating back to Napoleonic times complement the gracious service and talented culinary staff.

PREPARATION

1. Grapefruit Compote. Peel grapefruits, divide into segments, and remove membrane. In medium saucepan, combine all ingredients except grapefruit and cook for 30 minutes. Add grapefruit segments, cook 2 minutes, remove from heat, and keep warm.

2. Cilantro-Lime Vinaigrette. Mix all ingredients in small bowl.

3. Fried Spinach. Heat at least 2 inches of oil in deep skillet or heavy-bottomed pot. Add spinach and cook until crisp. Remove and place on paper towels, patting with fresh towels to absorb excess oil. If wilted spinach is preferred, cook in only 1 tablespoon oil, until wilted, and do not dry with towels.

4. Sesame Seed-Crusted Bass. Preheat oven to 350 degrees. Combine sesame seeds and ginger in shallow dish and roll bass in mixture. Heat ovenproof pan over medium heat, add fish, and sear. Place pan in oven and bake fish for 10–15 minutes, or longer if necessary.

5. Serving. Spoon vinaigrette on bottom of each plate, top with fried or wilted spinach, put grapefruit compote on right side of plate, and fish on left side.

JEFFERY L. ERICKSON

GRILLED SALMON WITH SHIITAKE MUSHROOM SAUCE, WHITE BEAN MOUSSE AND WILTED SPINACH

SERVES: 4

PREPARATION: 30 minutes
(uncooked beans require overnight
to soak and 2 hours to cook)

COOKING: 15 minutes

240 Union
240 Union Boulevard
Lakewood, Colorado 80228
(303) 989-3562

240 Union wins applause for
"creative" new American fare.
The contemporary, casual
setting is first class, from patio
to dining room. Enjoy roasted
sea bass with black olive crust,
lamb chops with rosemary
mustard aioli, or gourmet
pizza prepared in applewood-
burning ovens.

MATTHEW FRANKLIN

Shiitake Mushroom Sauce
2 tablespoons minced shallots
1 cup sliced shiitake mushrooms
3 tablespoons butter
½ cup dry red wine
¼ cup tomato purée
1 cup beef stock
Salt and pepper to taste

White Bean Mousse
4 ounces bacon, cut into small pieces
1 medium onion, chopped
1 cup heavy cream
4 cups cooked white beans, drained
Salt and pepper to taste
¼ cup butter, cut into pieces

Salmon
4 6-ounce salmon fillets
Salt and pepper
2 tablespoons olive oil

Wilted Spinach
3 tablespoons olive oil
1 tablespoon minced garlic
4 cups lightly packed fresh spinach
Salt and pepper to taste
1 lemon, juice only

PREPARATION

1. Shiitake Mushroom Sauce. Sauté shallots and mushrooms in butter until golden, add wine, and cook until liquid is reduced by two thirds. Add tomato purée and beef stock and cook until reduced by one third. Season with salt and pepper and keep warm.

2. White Bean Mousse. Sauté bacon over medium heat until lightly browned, add onions, lower heat, and cook slowly until onions are soft. Add cream, bring to a boil, stir in beans, and heat through. Season with salt and pepper. Transfer to food processor and blend, adding butter 1 piece at a time, until smooth. Keep warm.

3. Salmon. Season fish with salt and pepper, brush with oil, and grill until medium-rare. Fish should be springy to touch and slightly translucent in center. Keep warm.

4. Wilted Spinach. Heat large pan, add oil, garlic, and spinach and sauté, stirring until spinach is lightly wilted and bright green in color. Season with salt and pepper and lemon juice.

5. Serving. Spoon equal portions of sauce on warm plates, arrange mound of spinach on each plate, and top with white bean mousse, then salmon.

NOTE

• Advanced preparation is required for uncooked beans.

STEAMED SALMON WITH GLAZED ENDIVES IN A RED WINE SAUCE

Red Wine Sauce
2 shallots, finely chopped
½ cup unsalted butter
1 cup red wine
Salt and pepper to taste

Endives
2 Belgium endives
1 tablespoon unsalted butter
2 tablespoons sugar

Salmon
1 cup white wine
4 6-ounce salmon fillets

SERVES: 4
PREPARATION: 10 minutes
COOKING: 20 minutes

PREPARATION

1. Red Wine Sauce. In small saucepan, sauté shallots in 1 teaspoon of the butter. Add wine and cook until liquid is reduced by half. Cut remaining butter in pieces and whisk in butter, 1 piece at a time. Season with salt and pepper if necessary.

2. Endives. Separate leaves and sauté endives in butter and sugar until caramelized. (Endives will begin to wilt and will be coated with sugar.)

3. Salmon. In large covered skillet or pan, bring wine to boil, add salmon and steam covered until fish is cooked. Fish should be springy to the touch with a slightly translucent center.

4. Serving. Arrange endives on each plate in form of a star (about 5 leaves per plate). Place salmon fillet in center and top with wine sauce. Serve immediately.

NOTE

• For those on restricted diets, omit the butter in the red wine sauce. The sauce will be somewhat stronger in flavor.

Mirabelle at Beaver Creek Restaurant

Mirabelle at Beaver Creek
55 Village Road
Beaver Creek, Colorado 81620
(970) 949-7728

Located in a hundred-year-old landmark building, Mirabelle is a nationally acclaimed restaurant. Chef Daniel Joly creates distinctive dishes with a Belgian accent. Homemade pastries and breads, plus an extensive wine list, complement each creation.

DANIEL JOLY

STEAMED SEA BASS WITH GINGER SAUCE

Steamed Bass
4 6- to 8-ounce striped sea bass fillets
2 tablespoons peeled, fresh gingerroot
8–10 scallions, white sections, julienned

Sauce
¼ cup soy sauce
1 cup water
½ teaspoon sugar
Sesame oil
Ground white pepper

SERVES: 4
PREPARATION: 5 minutes
COOKING: 20 minutes

⬖ IMPERIAL

The Imperial
431 South Broadway
Denver, Colorado 80209
(303) 698-2800

The Imperial Chinese
Restaurant is an elegant,
fine-dining establishment
featuring the food of the
Szechuan, Mandarin, Hunan,
and Cantonese provinces.
The modern decor is enhanced
by the delicate flavors, rich colors,
and textures of each dish.

PREPARATION

1. Steamed Bass. In large skillet with cover, bring enough water to cover fish to a boil. Add fish, cover, and steam for 10–15 minutes, depending on size of fish. Fish should be springy to the touch with a slightly translucent center. Transfer fish to a plate and top with ginger and scallions.

2. Sauce. In small saucepan, combine soy sauce, water, and sugar. Bring to a boil, stirring continuously, and pour over fish. Add a few drops of oil and a sprinkling of pepper. Serve immediately.

NOTE

• This dish works well for any type of bass.

GEORGE YU

SWORDFISH LAYERED WITH SPINACH AND BLACK BEAN POLENTA

Black Bean Polenta
1 cup cooked black beans
1 red onion, diced
1 yellow bell pepper, seeded and diced
1 scallion, diced
¼ bunch fresh cilantro, diced
2 cups water
½ cup polenta
    (coarsely ground cornmeal)
2 tablespoons buttermilk
2 tablespoons grated smoked mozzarella

Swordfish
1 lime, juice only
½ teaspoon cayenne pepper
1 teaspoon each paprika, chili powder,
    and ground cumin
¼ cup olive oil
4 swordfish steaks, cut in half lengthwise

Yellow Pepper Sauce
1 yellow bell pepper, seeded and chopped
1 clove garlic
1 pinch minced thyme
1 pinch minced rosemary
1 cup unsalted chicken stock

Spinach
1 teaspoon olive oil
1 pound spinach
1 lime, juice only

SERVES: 4

PREPARATION: 20 minutes
(uncooked beans require overnight
soaking and 2 hours to cook;
polenta cools 4–6 hours.)

COOKING: 25 minutes

Cliff Young's

Cliff Young's
700 East Seventeenth Avenue
Denver, Colorado 80203
(303) 831-8900

*Cliff Young's is Denver's answer
to elegant fine dining. With
the romantic, richly decorated
Amethyst Room, the stately
Crystal Room, or the nonpareil
main dining room, Cliff Young's
is a truly wonderful epicurean
experience.*

PREPARATION

1. Black Bean Polenta. Cook beans according to package instructions.
Place onions, yellow pepper, scallions, cilantro, and water in large pot, bring to a boil,
and simmer 5 minutes. Add drained beans and cornmeal and cook 15 minutes.
Polenta should be very thick, not runny. Stir in buttermilk and cheese, spread mixture
into loaf pan, and cool 4–6 hours. When ready to serve, slice into 1 inch pieces and
heat in 350 degree oven for approximately 10 minutes.

2. Swordfish. Combine all ingredients, except fish, in shallow nonreactive dish.
Add fish and marinate 15 minutes. When ready to serve, grill swordfish for 3–5 minutes
on each side. Fish should be springy to touch with a slightly translucent center.

3. Yellow Pepper Sauce. Combine all ingredients in small saucepan and
simmer 15 minutes. Transfer to food processor or blender, purée until smooth, strain,
and keep warm.

4. Spinach. Heat oil in a medium sauté pan, add spinach and lime juice,
and sear.

5. Serving. Pour small amount of sauce on each plate, place polenta in center,
and top with 1 swordfish half. Then place enough spinach on top to cover the fish and
top with the remaining swordfish half.

SEAN BRASEL

SWORDFISH WITH HOISIN BUTTER

Hoisin Butter
¼ pound unsalted butter, softened
4–6 tablespoons Hoisin sauce

Garnish
30 golden raisins
30 banana slices
24 chive spears
¼ cup sake

Swordfish
6 7-ounce swordfish steaks,
    approximately ¾-inch thick
⅓ cup sesame seeds
Olive oil for sautéing

PREPARATION

1. Hoisin Butter. Place butter in food processor or blender and mix until smooth. Add Hoisin, beginning with 4 tablespoons, and blend until well mixed. (The Hoisin should be quite strong. It lessens when it melts on the fish.) Refrigerate if not used immediately. Bring to room temperature to serve.

2. Garnish. Place raisins in small sauté pan, barely cover with sake, and poach gently until sake evaporates. Place five banana slices around edge of each plate and top each slice with 1 raisin. To complete the design, create a box inside banana-raisin ring using chive spears. The swordfish will be placed in the center.

3. Swordfish. Coat 1 side of swordfish with sesame seeds. Heat oil in large sauté pan, add fish, and sauté until medium. Do not overcook. The center of fish should be slightly translucent.

4. Serving. Place swordfish in center of plate. Using pastry bag, pipe 1 tablespoon Hoisin butter onto fish. If pastry bag is not available, spoon butter onto fish.

SERVES: 6
PREPARATION: 25 minutes
COOKING: 5 minutes

Soupçon
127 A Elk Avenue
Crested Butte, Colorado 81224
(970) 349-5448

Soupçon offers a warm country atmosphere in an intimate setting—there are only nine tables in this gem of the Rockies. Chef-owner Mac Bailey's mission is to "use the freshest ingredients, start from scratch, and make good food."

MAC BAILEY

TAMARI-GLAZED SWORDFISH
WITH BANANA-LEMON-GINGER CHUTNEY,
SAUTÉED SHIITAKE MUSHROOMS AND WATERCRESS

Banana-Lemon-Ginger Chutney

½ white onion, finely diced

Olive oil

2 teaspoons peeled, minced gingerroot

1 tablespoon peanut oil

¼ cup brown sugar

3 medium-sized, almost-ripe bananas,
   cut in to 1-inch pieces

1 lemon, juice only

2 tablespoons sherry vinegar

2 tablespoons orange juice

1 small anaheim chili, roasted,
   peeled, seeded, and chopped

Pinch each of ground cloves,
   5 spice powder, and ground star anise

Salt and pepper to taste

Swordfish

¼ cup tamari

1 tablespoon honey

2 5-ounce swordfish steaks

Shiitake Mushrooms and Watercress

4 tablespoons peanut oil

2 cups julienned shiitakes

½ cup very dry sherry

2 tablespoons tamari (or soy sauce)

4 tablespoons butter, cut into cubes

15–20 sprigs watercress

Garnish

Zest of 2 lemons

Toasted sesame seeds

SERVES: 2

PREPARATION: 40 minutes
(chutney sits overnight)

COOKING: 25 minutes

たか

TAKAH SUSHI

Takah Sushi
420 East Hyman Avenue
Aspen, Colorado 81611
(970) 925-8588

*Takah Sushi features Japanese-
accented cuisine ranging from
Tamari-glazed swordfish to
vegetarian sushi rolls. Patrons
marvel at the skill and art of
sushi preparation while enjoying
delectable, exquisitely presented
creations.*

PREPARATION

1. Banana-Lemon-Ginger Chutney. Make at least 1 day ahead. Sauté onions
in small amount of olive oil for 3 minutes; do not brown. Add gingerroot and sauté for
2–3 minutes. Add remaining ingredients and cook over medium heat for 10–15 minutes,
or until consistency is somewhat like ketchup. Cool.

2. Swordfish. Mix tamari and honey in small bowl. Grill swordfish over
medium heat, brushing occasionally with tamari-and-honey mixture.

3. Shiitake Mushrooms and Watercress. In large skillet, heat peanut oil,
add shiitakes, and sauté 1 minute. Add sherry, stirring to dissolve any sautéed particles
remaining in the pan. Add butter and tamari or soy sauce, but do not boil for more
than 30 seconds. Add watercress sprigs and turn off heat.

4. Serving. Spoon shiitake-watercress sauce over bottom of each plate,
covering entire surface. Place swordfish in center, top with 3 tablespoons chutney,
and garnish with light sprinkling of lemon zest and sesame seeds.

Kathy B. Sisson
KATHY B. SISSON

THAI LOBSTER WITH JASMINE RICE

Jasmine Rice
2 cups cooked jasmine rice

Lobster
4 1½-pound lobsters
2 tablespoons butter

Curry Sauce
1 tablespoon butter
1½ teaspoons curry paste
⅓ medium carrot, julienned
Salt and pepper to taste
1 tablespoon port
¼ apple, peeled, cored, and julienned
½ teaspoon turmeric
¼ cup heavy cream
1 tablespoon chopped fresh cilantro

SERVES: 4
PREPARATION: 15 minutes
COOKING: 20–25 minutes

PREPARATION

1. Jasmine Rice. Cook according to package directions, usually about 20 minutes.

2. Lobster. Bring large pot of water to a boil, add lobsters, and blanch 2 minutes. Remove lobster meat from shells, trying to keep pieces in tact, and sauté in butter 2 minutes. Set aside.

3. Curry Sauce. In saucepan over medium heat, melt butter, add curry paste, and stir until blended. Add carrots, pinch of salt, and port, stirring continuously. Add apple and cook until mixture is almost dry. Stir in turmeric and cream, bring to a boil, and remove from heat. Add cilantro and salt and pepper.

4. Serving. Place lobster meat in center of plate, encircle with jasmine rice and top with sauce.

European Cafe

European Cafe
2460 Arapahoe Avenue
Boulder, Colorado 80302
(303) 938-8250
and
1515 Market Street
Denver, Colorado 80202
(303) 825-6555

Chef Radek Cerny immigrated to the United States from Czechoslovakia. In 1989, a dream was realized with the opening of the European Cafe in Boulder. Here the best elements of continental cuisine and healthy food are combined in an elegant setting with unrushed service.

RADEK CERNY

CHICKEN AND SAUSAGE STEW OVER GRILLED POLENTA

Polenta

4 cups water

1 teaspoon salt

1¼ cups polenta
(coarsely ground cornmeal)

⅔ cup freshly grated Parmesan cheese

Chicken and Sausage Stew

6 chicken legs and thighs

All-purpose flour seasoned with
salt and pepper

¼ cup olive oil

½ pound large link sausage,
cut in 1-inch pieces

⅓ cup chopped carrots

⅓ cup chopped celery

⅓ cup chopped onions

½ cup dry white wine

⅓ cup canned Italian tomatoes, chopped

1 tablespoon chopped fresh sage

1 teaspoon minced fresh thyme

1 cup chicken stock or water

Garnish

Fresh sage leaves

SERVES: 4

PREPARATION: 20 minutes
(polenta is refrigerated for 6 hours)

COOKING: 40 minutes

Campagna
435 West Pacific Avenue
Telluride, Colorado 81435
(970) 728-6190

*Campagna serves country food
from Tuscany, the heart of
northern Italy. Using only the
finest ingredients, Chef-owner
Vincent Esposito prepares food
that* Bon Appetit *magazine has
called "sophisticated yet homey."
You'll feel like you stepped into
a Tuscan country home.*

PREPARATION

1. Polenta. Bring water and salt to a boil. Add polenta in thin stream, stirring constantly. Reduce heat to low simmer and continue stirring until thick. Add cheese, pour into a 8x4x4-inch loaf pan, and cool. Refrigerate 6 hours. When ready to serve, cut polenta into ½-inch-thick slices and grill for approximately 8 minutes per side.

2. Chicken and Sausage Stew. Skin and debone chicken. Cut into 2x3-inch pieces, dredge in flour, and shake off excess. Heat oil in large sauté pan, add chicken, and sauté until browned on both sides. Transfer to paper towels and keep warm.

In same pan over medium heat, cook sausage until browned. Drain any excess fat, add carrots, celery, and onions, and cook until vegetables begin to soften, about 10 minutes. Increase heat to high, add wine, and cook until liquid is reduced by half. Add tomatoes, chicken, sage, thyme, and chicken stock or water. Bring to a boil, reduce heat, and simmer until stew thickens, approximately 30 minutes. If needed, add more liquid. Season with salt to taste.

3. Serving. Place 2 slices of polenta on each plate, top with stew, and garnish with sage leaves.

NOTE

• Polenta can be made the day before.

VINCENT ESPOSITO

POACHED BREAST OF CHICKEN WITH CITRUS-GARLIC SAUCE

SERVES: 4
PREPARATION: 10 minutes
COOKING: 20–25 minutes

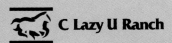

C Lazy U Ranch
P.O. Box 379
Granby, Colorado 80446
(970) 887-3344

C Lazy U Ranch, one of the country's outstanding guest ranches, has received both Mobil's five-star and AAA's five-diamond awards for the past thirteen years. Guests dine overlooking a breathtaking expanse of mountains and meadows. Summer or winter, C Lazy U Ranch is an experience of a lifetime.

Citrus-Garlic Sauce
2½ cups chicken stock
10 garlic cloves, sliced
1 tablespoon chopped fresh dill
3 tablespoons orange juice concentrate
4 grapefruit segments, membranes removed

Poached Breast of Chicken
4 4- to 5-ounce boneless, skinless chicken breasts

Garnish
1 red bell pepper, julienned

PREPARATION

1. Citrus-Garlic Sauce. Place all ingredients in large sauté pan, bring to a boil, reduce heat to low, and simmer for 10 minutes.

2. Poached Breast of Chicken. Place chicken breasts in sauté pan with sauce and poach covered on one side for 4–5 minutes. Turn chicken over and poach covered for an additional 3 minutes or until done. Remove chicken breasts and keep warm.

Increase heat to high and cook sauce 4 minutes or until it thickens. Strain, reserving sauce.

3. Serving. Place chicken on individual plates, top with sauce, and garnish with bell peppers.

STEPHEN REYNOLDS

SMOKED CHICKEN AND WILD MUSHROOM BURRITO

Smoked Chicken and Wild Mushroom Filling
2 tablespoons olive oil
2 ounces oyster mushrooms, chopped
2 ounces shiitake mushrooms, chopped
2 garlic cloves, minced
2 tablespoons chopped fresh cilantro
6 ounces smoked chicken, diced
2 tablespoons tequila
½ teaspoon cayenne pepper
½ teaspoon each salt and pepper
2 tablespoons diced green chilies
½ cup chicken or veal stock

Burrito
1 cup refried beans
8 soft tortillas
¼ pound shredded Monterey Jack cheese

Garnish
Sour cream (optional)

SERVES: 8
PREPARATION: 20 minutes
COOKING: 10 minutes

Tall Timber

Tall Timber
Box 90
Silverton Star Route
Durango, Colorado 81301
(970) 259-4813

Tall Timber, located in a wilderness setting in the heart of the San Juan Mountains, pampers its guests with five-star and five-diamond service. No roads lead to this luxury retreat; all guests arrive on either the narrow-gauge railroad or helicopter to enjoy international cuisine and a variety of activities.

PREPARATION

1. Smoked Chicken and Wild Mushroom Filling. Heat oil in large skillet and sauté mushrooms. Stir in garlic, cilantro, and chicken. Add tequila, cayenne, and salt and pepper, stirring until well mixed. Add chilies and stock and stir.

2. Burrito. Heat refried beans, place beans in center of each tortilla, and top with 2–3 tablespoons filling. Sprinkle with cheese and roll up.

3. Serving. Place burrito on each plate and top with a teaspoon of sour cream.

NOTES

• If smoked chicken is not available, use 6 ounces of regular chicken and substitute smoked mozzarella cheese for Monterey Jack.

• All manner of tortillas are available in health-food stores, specialty markets, and large grocery stores. Try this recipe with vegetarian tortillas or any other that suits your fancy.

DENNIS J. SHAKAN

HONEY PECAN CHICKEN

Honey Cream Sauce
2 tablespoons butter
1 tablespoon minced shallots
1 cup fresh orange juice
¼ cup bourbon
1 cup whipping cream
2 tablespoons honey
1 tablespoon cider vinegar
Salt and pepper to taste

Pecan Chicken
¼ cup all-purpose flour
1 teaspoon minced fresh thyme
¼ cup finely chopped pecans
Salt and pepper to taste
6 boneless, skinless chicken breast halves
Olive oil for sautéing

PREPARATION

1. Honey Cream Sauce. Heat butter in medium saucepan, add shallots, and cook over low heat 3–4 minutes or until tender but not brown. Add orange juice and bourbon, increase heat, and continue cooking until liquid is reduced to ½ cup. Add cream and reduce until slightly thickened. Add honey and vinegar and season with salt and pepper.

2. Pecan Chicken. Mix flour, thyme, pecans, and salt and pepper. Dredge chicken breasts in flour mixture. Heat a small amount of oil in a large sauté pan, add chicken, and sauté until golden brown.

3. Serving. Pour sauce onto each plate and place chicken breast in center. Serve additional sauce separately.

SERVES: 6
PREPARATION: 10 minutes
COOKING: 20–25 minutes

The Home Ranch
54880 Route 129
Clark, Colorado 80428
(970) 879-1780

Located at the northern end of the breathtaking Elk River Valley, The Home Ranch, offers a gracious combination of western warmth, creature comforts, and lively outdoor activities. Rarely repeating a meal during the year has earned The Home Ranch both Mobil's four-star and AAA's four-diamond awards.

CLYDE R. NELSON

DUCK BREAST WITH APRICOT SAUCE

1 cup unsalted chicken stock
½ cup dried apricots
1 tablespoon olive oil
4 boneless, skinless duck breast halves
2 tablespoons brandy or cognac
Salt and pepper to taste

SERVES: 4
PREPARATION: 5 minutes
COOKING: 25 minutes

PREPARATION

Simmer chicken stock until reduced to ¼ cup and set aside. Place apricots in separate saucepan, cover with water, and simmer until soft. Strain, reserving ½ cup liquid. Purée apricots and reserved apricot liquid in blender or food processor until smooth.

In large sauté pan, heat oil and sauté duck breasts until medium-rare, approximately 10 minutes. Remove from pan and keep warm. Add reduced chicken stock to sauté pan, stirring to dissolve any particles in bottom of pan. Add apricot purée and brandy or cognac. Reduce until sauce thickens slightly and salt and pepper to taste. To serve, slice duck breast diagonally, fan meat on individual plate and top with sauce.

NOTE

• This recipe is also good with pheasant and chicken.

La Petite Maison
1015 West Colorado Avenue
Colorado Springs, Colorado 80904
(719) 632-4887

Located in a an old Victorian home, La Petite Maison is a small, intimate restaurant where the cuisine is a tender balance of classic cooking and innovative creation. The wine list is as outstanding as the cuisine.

Holly B. Mervis
HOLLY B. MERVIS

CORNISH GAME HENS WITH
PHEASANT SAUSAGE STUFFING AND RED ONION MARMALADE

Pheasant Sausage
¾ pound pheasant meat *(see Notes)*
½ pound bacon
2 tablespoons chili powder
1 tablespoon paprika
1 teaspoon salt
1 tablespoon pepper
1 teaspoon ground cumin
1½ teaspoons ground nutmeg
½ teaspoon minced fresh cilantro
2 cloves garlic
2 scallions, chopped
¼ teaspoon chili flakes or
  red pepper flakes
¼ red bell pepper, rough cut
1 tablespoon sugar

Cornish Game Hens
4 Cornish game hens

Red Onion Marmalade
1 red onion, julienned
½ red bell pepper, julienned
2 green bell peppers, julienned
½ Anaheim chili, julienned
½ lemon, juice and zest
½ orange, juice and zest
½ lime, juice only
1 cup honey
1 cup light Karo syrup
½ teaspoon ground nutmeg
½ teaspoon ground cinnamon
1 packet gelatine or pectin

SERVES: 4
PREPARATION: 25 minutes
COOKING: 1 hour, 30 minutes

Palace Arms
The Brown Palace Hotel
321 Seventeenth Street
Denver, Colorado 80202
(303) 297-3111

Denver's only Mobil four-star restaurant, the Palace Arms' elegant atmosphere and contemporary cuisine combine for a memorable dining experience. Stained glass, objets d'art, and antiques dating back to Napoleonic times complement the gracious service and talented culinary staff

PREPARATION

1. Pheasant Sausage. Preheat oven to 350 degrees. Combine all ingredients in food processor or grinder until roughly mixed.

2. Cornish Game Hens. Rinse hens and pat dry. Stuff with pheasant sausage and bake for 1–1½ hours or until done.

3. Red Onion Marmalade. Combine all ingredients in medium saucepan, bring to a boil, reduce heat, and simmer until mixture thickens, approximately 1 hour.

4. Serving. Cut each hen in half, place 2 halves on each plate, and top with red onion marmalade.

NOTES

• Duck meat can be substituted for the pheasant meat.
• Made with quail, this recipe works well as an appetizer.
• The pheasant bones can be used in the recipe for Cider and Onion Soup with Smoked Mozzarella Croutons (page 34).

Jeffrey L. Erickson
JEFFREY L. ERICKSON

GRILLED SQUAB WITH TOMATOES AND GRITS

SERVES: 4
PREPARATION: 30 minutes
COOKING: 2 hours, 40 minutes

The Wildflower
The Lodge at Vail
174 East Gore Creek Drive
Vail, Colorado 81657
(970) 476-5011
(800) 331-LODG

Creative American cuisine and terraced views of Vail Mountain combine for spectacular gourmet dining in timeless elegance at The Wildflower. Chef Jim Cohen's innovative fare has received national recognition from Mobil Travel Guide, AAA, *the James Beard Foundation, and* Travel/Holiday *magazine.*

JAMES E. COHEN

Sauce
Squab bones
   (from deboning breasts)
½ medium onion, rough cut
½ head garlic, crushed
4 cups unsalted chicken stock
1 sprig fresh parsley
3 sprigs fresh basil

Squab
1 cup olive oil
3 tablespoons honey
4 sprigs fresh thyme
1 clove garlic, crushed
2 teaspoons freshly ground black pepper
4 squab breasts, skinned and deboned
   (save bones for sauce)

Tomatoes
4 tomatoes, peeled
Salt and pepper to taste

Grits
1 cup grits

PREPARATION

1. Sauce. Preheat oven to 400 degrees. Place squab bones, onions, and garlic in pan and roast until golden brown. Transfer to stock pot, add chicken stock, and bring to a boil. Reduce heat and simmer uncovered 2 hours. Add parsley and basil and continue simmering for 30 minutes more. Pour through fine-mesh strainer, return to pot, and cook until liquid is reduced by half.

2. Squab. Mix oil, honey, thyme, crushed garlic, and black pepper in shallow dish, and marinate squab breasts for 30 minutes. When everything else is almost ready, grill squab breasts until medium-rare.

3. Tomatoes. Cut tomatoes in half, season with salt and pepper, and bake for 10 minutes.

4. Grits. Cook according to package directions.

5. Serving. Spoon a serving of grits on each plate, top with 2 squab breasts, and place tomatoes halves to the side. Spoon sauce over squab breasts.

GRILLED VEAL CHOPS WITH TOMATO AND RED PEPPER SAUCE ON RED CHARD GRATIN

Tomato and Red Pepper Sauce

2 red bell peppers

4 tomatoes

1 tablespoon olive oil

1 small onion, chopped

1½ teaspoons crushed garlic

½ cup white wine

1 cup veal stock

½ teaspoon minced fresh rosemary

½ teaspoon chopped fresh thyme

Salt and pepper to taste

Red Chard Gratin

1 bunch red Swiss chard, rinsed and chopped

2 tablespoons butter

2 tablespoons all-purpose flour

1½ cups milk

4 ounces Gruyere cheese, grated

Salt and pepper to taste

Ground nutmeg to taste

Veal Chops

6–8 ounce veal chops

Garnish

2 tablespoons chopped pistachio nuts

SERVES: 4
PREPARATION: 15 minutes
COOKING: 45 minutes

La Marmotte
150 West San Juan Avenue
Telluride, Colorado 81435
(970) 728-6232

Hosts Bertrand Marchal and Noelle Lepel-Cointet transport France to the San Juan Mountains. At La Marmotte guests dine on outstanding classic and regional French cuisine. A romantic, cozy restaurant, it is an ideal place to linger over excellent wines in an unhurried, civilized oasis away from life's daily stresses.

PREPARATION

1. Tomato and Red Pepper Sauce. Grill or broil peppers until skin is charred. Remove and discard peel, seeds, and membrane. Chop into small pieces. Bring medium pot of water to a boil, add tomatoes, and cook 30 seconds. Remove from water and peel tomatoes. In large sauté pan, heat oil and sauté onions and garlic until translucent. Add tomatoes, bell peppers, wine, veal stock, rosemary, and thyme. Simmer for 30 minutes. Season with salt and pepper.

2. Red Chard Gratin. Bring medium pot of water to a boil, add chard, and cook until tender. Remove from heat, strain, and set aside. Return pan to heat, melt butter, add flour, and mix well. Slowly add milk, stirring continuously, and cook until thick. Add chard and cheese and season with salt, pepper, and nutmeg.

3. Veal Chops. Grill or broil until medium-rare.

4. Serving. Place chard gratin on each plate, arrange veal chops on top, pour sauce around the dish and garnish with pistachios.

NOTE

• Veal stock may be purchased from many local restaurants.

NÖELLE LEPEL-COINTET

BLACKENED PORK TENDERLOIN WITH APPLE AND ONION COMPOTE

SERVES: 8
PREPARATION: 25 minutes
COOKING: 2 hours

Piñons

Piñons
105 South Mill Street
Aspen, Colorado 81611
(970) 920-2021

Surrounded by turn-of-the-century paintings depicting the Wild West, diners are treated to "American cuisine with a Colorado touch." Patrons have been known to fly across the country for the elegant food expertly prepared by Chef Rob Mobilian.

ROBERT MOBILIAN

Pork Sauce
½ pound pork bones
1 tablespoons rough-cut shallots
1½ teaspoons minced garlic
5 peppercorns
1 bay leaf
½ cup Madeira wine
2 cups veal stock *(see Note)*
1 tablespoon arrowroot

Apple and Onion Compote
4 tablespoons butter
3 red onions, finely chopped
8 Granny Smith apples,
    peeled, cored, and sliced
¼ cup brown sugar
1 teaspoon pâté spice
1 teaspoon ground cinnamon
½ cup Madeira wine
1 tablespoon chopped parsley
1 tablespoon chopped sage
½ cup veal stock
½ cup of the pork sauce
Salt and pepper to taste

Blackened Pork
8 8-ounce pork tenderloins
Salt (optional)
¼ cup blackened spice
2 tablespoons olive oil

PREPARATION

1. Pork Sauce. Bake pork bones in 400-degree oven until browned. Place bones in saucepan, add shallots, garlic, peppercorns, and bay leaf, and sauté 3 minutes. Add wine and veal stock and simmer uncovered 1 hour. Strain sauce and return to saucepan. Mix arrowroot with 3 tablespoons of water and pour into simmering sauce, mixing with a whisk. Keep warm.

2. Apple and Onion Compote. Melt butter in pan, add onions, and sauté until browned. Add apples, sugar, pâté spice, and cinnamon, and cook about 10 minutes or until apples just begin to soften. Add wine, parsley, sage, veal stock, and ½ cup of the pork sauce, stirring until thoroughly mixed. Season with salt and pepper and simmer 10 minutes. Keep warm.

3. Blackened Pork. Preheat oven to 400 degrees. Season tenderloins with salt, if desired, and coat with blackened spice. In ovenproof skillet, heat oil, add pork, and sear until deep dark red in color. Place skillet in oven and bake approximately 20–25 minutes or until medium-rare. Remove from oven and cut pork into slices.

4. Serving. Place apple and onion compote on each plate, fan pork slices on top of compote, and spoon on 2–4 tablespoons pork sauce.

NOTE

• Veal stock can be purchased from many local restaurants. If none is available, use unsalted beef broth.

ELK MEDALLIONS WITH CHANTERELLE RAGOUT AND BRUXELLES STOEMP

Bruxelles Stoemp

4 large potatoes, peeled and diced in 1-inch cubes

1 fresh fennel bulb, chopped

1 tablespoon unsalted butter

Salt and pepper to taste

Ground nutmeg to taste

Chanterelle Ragout

2 tablespoons butter, or 1 tablespoon olive oil and 1 tablespoon butter

3 shallots, finely chopped

6 ounces chanterelle mushrooms

½ cup port wine

Salt and pepper to taste

Elk Medallions

4 elk medallions *(see Notes)*

Salt and pepper

Olive oil for sautéing

SERVES: 4

PREPARATION: 20 minutes

COOKING: 40 minutes

Mirabelle at Beaver Creek Restaurant

Mirabelle at Beaver Creek
55 Village Road
Beaver Creek, Colorado 81620
(970) 949-7728

Located in a hundred-year-old landmark building, Mirabelle is a nationally acclaimed restaurant. Chef Daniel Joly creates distinctive dishes with a Belgian accent. Homemade pastries and breads, plus an extensive wine list, complement each creation.

PREPARATION

1. Bruxelles Stoemp. Place potatoes and fennel in large pot, cover with water, and cook until water is completely evaporated. Mash together, add butter, salt, pepper, and nutmeg.

2. Chanterelle Ragout. Heat 1 tablespoon butter or olive oil in sauté pan, add shallots and mushrooms, and cook approximately 2 minutes over medium heat. Stir in port and cook until liquid is reduced by half. Remove from heat, add 1 tablespoon cold butter and stir. Season with salt and pepper.

3. Elk. Season elk with salt and pepper. Heat oil in sauté pan, add elk, and sauté until medium-rare, approximately 2 minutes per side.

4. Serving. Place elk in center of plate, top with mushrooms, and place stoemp to one side.

NOTES

• If chanterelle mushrooms are unavailable, shiitake mushrooms may be substituted.

• Elk can be purchased from many butchers. You may also contact Game Sales International (800-729-2090). They ship, overnight, throughout the United States.

DANIEL JOLY

GRILLED ELK TENDERLOIN ON A COMPOTE OF POTATOES, CABBAGE AND MUSHROOMS WITH SUNDRIED CHERRY SAUCE AND SWEET POTATO CROQUETTES

SERVES: 6

PREPARATION: 40 minutes
(elk and croquettes refrigerate overnight)
COOKING: 25 minutes

THE LITTLE NELL

Restaurant at The Little Nell
The Little Nell
675 East Durant Street
Aspen, Colorado 81611
(970) 920-4600

*The Restaurant at The Little Nell
combines European ambiance
with a Rocky Mountain setting
—the ultimate mountain getaway. Chef George Mahaffey
mixes regional foods with exotic
flavors, creating dishes that
have won the restaurant
Mobil's four-star and AAA's
four-diamond awards.*

GEORGE MAHAFFEY

Elk Loin

3 pounds elk loin, denuded *(see Notes)*

3 tablespoons each, chopped fresh
   parsley and thyme

Sweet Potato Croquettes

2 cups peeled, sliced sweet potatoes

1 tablespoon maple syrup

1 teaspoon chopped chives

1 teaspoon chopped fresh thyme

4 tablespoons unsalted butter

¼ cup cream

2 eggs

½ cup powdered instant potatoes

Potato Compote

1 cup peeled, diced potatoes
   (about ½-inch dice)

1 cup chicken stock

1½ cups sliced Napa cabbage

1½ cups sliced mushrooms

1 cup cream

Salt and pepper to taste

Sundried Cherry Sauce

1 cup sundried cherries

1 cup apple juice

1 cup cranberry juice

1 shallot, peeled and sliced

1 clove garlic

1 cinnamon stick

1 whole clove

1 small bay leaf

10 peppercorns

6 sprigs fresh thyme

Champagne Vinaigrette

1 teaspoon Dijon mustard

½ teaspoon salt

1 teaspoon chopped shallots

4 tablespoons champagne vinegar

1 teaspoon chopped fresh chives

¾–1 cup canola oil

½ teaspoon black pepper

Salad Greens

1 pound mixed greens

PREPARATION

1. Elk. Cut elk loin into 12 pieces, about 4 ounces each. Lightly pound to ¾-inch thickness. Coat elk with parsley and thyme mixture and refrigerate overnight.

2. Sweet Potato Croquettes. Cook sweet potatoes in water until soft. Drain and place in large bowl. Whip until smooth, add remaining ingredients, and blend well. Place mixture in saucepan and cook over low heat until thickened, stirring constantly. Refrigerate overnight. Form croquettes into hamburger-shaped patties and refrigerate until serving time.

3. Potato Compote. Combine potatoes and chicken stock in medium saucepan and cook until stock is completely evaporated; transfer to bowl. Add remaining ingredients to saucepan, bring to a boil, and cook 5 minutes. Strain and return liquid to saucepan. Continue cooking until very thick. Combine with potato mixture, season with salt and pepper, and set aside to cool.

4. Sundried Cherry Sauce. Combine cherries and juices in saucepan. Wrap remaining ingredients in cheesecloth and tie to close. Add to cherry mixture, simmer 15 minutes, then remove and discard bag. Purée mixture in blender or food processor and strain. Sauce should measure approximately 2 cups. If it greatly exceeds 2 cups, return to saucepan and reduce. Keep warm.

5. Champagne Vinaigrette. Combine all ingredients in bowl and whisk to blend.

6. Serving. Grill elk loin. (Elk is very lean and will dry out if cooked more than medium. It is best served medium-rare.) Fry croquettes about 1 minute in oil at 350 degrees. Remove from pan and drain on paper towels. Heat potato compote and spoon approximately ⅓ cup in center of each plate. Place 2 elk medallions on top of compote, and drizzle 4 tablespoons sauce around perimeter of each plate. Toss greens with ¼ cup vinaigrette, place on side of each plate, and arrange croquettes next to greens.

NOTES

- The sauces and croquettes can be made well in advance.
- Elk can be purchased from many butchers. You may also contact Game Sales International (800-729-2090). They ship, overnight, throughout the United States.

Lamb Shanks Braised in Zinfandel with Shiitake Mushrooms, Sundried Tomatoes and Seared Chard

SERVES: 6

PREPARATION: 20 minutes

COOKING: 2 hours

Q's
The Hotel Boulderado
2115 13th Street
Boulder, Colorado 80302
(303) 442-4880

Located on the mezzanine of the historic Hotel Boulderado, Q's serves contemporary American cuisine featuring foods indigenous to Colorado. An intimate atmosphere combined with unique culinary creations makes this spot one of the finest in the state.

Lamb Shanks

Olive oil

6 lamb shanks

2 tablespoons minced garlic

½ pound frozen pearl onions

¼ pound sundried tomatoes, halved

¾ pound shiitake mushrooms, stemmed and halved

2 cups Zinfandel wine

8 cups veal stock

2 bay leaves

Chard

1 bunch red Swiss chard

Olive oil

Salt and pepper to taste

PREPARATION

1. Lamb Shanks. Preheat oven to 375 degrees. Lightly coat bottom of roasting pan with oil and heat on stove top. Place shanks in oil and brown on all sides. Add garlic, onions, tomatoes, and mushrooms. When garlic becomes aromatic, stir in wine, stock, and bay leaves. Bring to a boil, cover, and place in oven for 2 hours. (Don't worry: you can't overcook them!) The meat should pull away from top of shanks and be extremely tender.

Remove shanks and strain liquid into small saucepan, saving vegetable mixture. Skim fat off surface of sauce. Return shanks, vegetables, and sauce to roasting pan and keep warm.

2. Chard. Wash chard and cut out center ribs. Julienne ribs and cut leaves into ¾-inch strips. Heat oil in sauté pan and when hot add chard. Sauté chard, adding a few drops of water to soften it, and season with salt and pepper.

3. Serving. Divide chard among the plates, prop a shank on each plate, and spoon vegetables and sauce on and around shank.

NOTES

• Ask the butcher to cut the knuckle end of the shanks flat so they can stand upright on a plate.

• Veal stock can be purchased from most local restaurants. If none is available, substitute unsalted beef broth.

JOHN PLATT

PINEY RIDGE ELK WITH
HERB DUMPLINGS AND JUNIPER PEACH RELISH

Juniper Peach Relish

1 pound ripe peaches,
    peeled, pitted, and roughly chopped

2 tablespoons olive oil

1 tablespoon crushed juniper berries

1 tablespoon lemon juice

2 teaspoons honey

½ teaspoon salt

¼ teaspoon white pepper

½ teaspoon Tabasco

Herb Dumplings

¼ cup mixed and minced arugula,
    fresh dill, and chives

½ cup buttermilk

2 eggs

1½ cups all-purpose flour

2 tablespoons butter, softened

1 tablespoon grated Parmesan cheese

1 teaspoon minced shallot

1 teaspoon sherry wine vinegar

1 teaspoon salt

¼ teaspoon white pepper

Pinch of cayenne

Pinch of dry mustard

Butter for sautéing

Elk

6 6-ounce elk loin steaks *(see Note)*

Salt and pepper

SERVES: 6
PREPARATION: 30 minutes
COOKING: 25 minutes

KEYSTONE RANCH

Keystone Ranch
1239 Keystone Ranch Road
Keystone, Colorado 80435
(970) 468-4130

*The Keystone Ranch is rich in
history of the Old West. Ute and
Arapaho Indians used the area
as their summer campground.
Today, guests dine on elegant
regional cuisine while seated in
a log cabin with views of the
Ten Mile and Gore Ranges.*

PREPARATION

1. Juniper Peach Relish. Mix all ingredients thoroughly in a bowl.

2. Herb Dumplings. Purée herbs and buttermilk in blender or food processor and transfer to bowl. Stir in remaining ingredients. Place in pastry bag with small or medium tip. Bring large pot of water to a boil and pipe mixture into boiling water. Remove as dumplings float to surface and drain on fine-mesh rack. Gently pat with paper towels to absorb excess moisture. Sauté dumplings in small amount of butter and season with salt and pepper.

3. Elk. Season elk with salt and pepper, then broil until rare to medium-rare. Cut elk on the bias.

4. Serving. Place small amount of dumplings on each plate and arrange elk on dumplings. Spoon relish over one corner of elk.

NOTE
• Elk can be purchased from many butchers. You may also contact Game Sales International (800-729-2090). They ship, overnight, throughout the United States.

CHRISTOPHER WING

PAN-ROASTED BUFFALO STEAK WITH BARBECUED ROCKY MOUNTAIN SHIITAKE MUSHROOMS AND CHEESE GRITS

Sweet and Spicy Barbecue Sauce
1 dry ancho pepper
1 dry New Mexico red chili
½ chipolte pepper
2 cloves garlic
1 bay leaf
1½ cups tomato juice
¼ cup balsamic vinegar
½ cup orange juice
¼ cup molasses
6 cups unsalted chicken stock

Cheese Grits
2½ cups unsalted chicken stock
½ small white onion, minced
1 cup white hominy grits
½ cup Monterey Jack cheese, grated
¼ cup grated sharp white cheddar cheese
1 tablespoon chopped fresh thyme

Buffalo Steaks
2 tablespoons olive oil
4 6-ounce sirloin or flank steaks
1 pound shiitake mushrooms, sliced
1 cup sweet and spicy barbecue sauce

SERVES: 4
PREPARATION: 30 minutes
COOKING: 30 minutes

Tante Louise
4900 East Colfax Avenue
Denver, Colorado 80220
(303) 355-4488

Situated in a renovated Victorian bungalow with hardwood floors, candlelit tables, and glowing fireplaces, Tante Louise is a AAA four-diamond restaurant. It features contemporary French-American fare with an impressive selection of more than 350 domestic and imported wines.

PREPARATION

1. Sweet and Spicy Barbecue Sauce. Remove stems and seeds from peppers. Place all ingredients in medium pan and simmer until peppers are soft. Purée in blender or food processor and pour through fine-mesh strainer or cheesecloth.

2. Cheese Grits. Simmer chicken stock and onions in medium pan for 10 minutes. Whisk in grits and cook 5 minutes. Stir in remaining ingredients. Remove from heat and keep warm.

3. Buffalo Steaks. Heat oil in large sauté pan, add steaks, and cook to personal preference. Remove from pan and keep warm. Add shiitake mushrooms to pan and sauté for 3–4 minutes or until soft. Add barbecue sauce and sauté 2 minutes.

4. Serving. Place steak and grits on each plate and spoon mushrooms around steaks.

NOTES

• The barbecue sauce makes approximately 8 cups. It will keep in the refrigerator for 1 week, or can be frozen. It is very good with seafood, such as shrimp or swordfish.

• Chopped fresh cilantro makes a nice garnish. Use about ¼ cup.

MICHAEL DEGENHART

VEAL L'APOGÉE

SERVES: 8
PREPARATION: 15 minutes
COOKING: 15 minutes

L'apogée
911 Lincoln Avenue
Steamboat Springs, Colorado 80477
(970) 879-1919

*Stained glass, objets d'art, and
fresh flowers create an intimate,
romantic atmosphere at L'apogée.
French cuisine with an Asian flare,
an exceptional, award-winning wine
list, and superb service transport Old
World elegance to Steamboat Springs.*

Veal
¼ cup all-purpose flour
1 teaspoon salt
2 teaspoons white pepper
1½ pounds veal top round,
　　thinly sliced and pounded to ⅛ inch
1 tablespoon butter
1 teaspoon finely chopped shallots

*Mushroom, Tomato and
Artichoke Sauce*
¼ cup cognac
4 ounces chanterelle mushrooms, sliced
3 artichoke bottoms, sliced
⅓ cup heavy cream
2 tablespoons demi-glaze *(see Notes)*
¼ cup peeled, seeded, and diced
　　Roma tomatoes
Salt and pepper to taste
¼ cup diced green onions

PREPARATION

1. Veal. Sift flour and mix in salt and pepper. Lightly dredge veal in flour mixture. Melt butter in large skillet, add shallots and veal, and sauté until veal is almost done (it should be slightly pink in the center). Remove and keep warm.

2. Mushroom, Tomato and Artichoke Sauce. Return same skillet to stove, add cognac and ignite by touching match to pan (be very careful, for flames can be high). Add chanterelles and artichokes and when cognac has almost evaporated, add cream and demi-glaze. Simmer for 4–5 minutes. As sauce thickens add tomatoes and season with salt and pepper. Sprinkle with green onions right before removing from heat.

3. Serving. Divide veal among six warm plates and top with sauce.

NOTES

• Demi-glaze is a meat glaze made by reducing beef or veal stock. It can be purchased from most local restaurants. Simmering 1 cup of unsalted beef broth until reduced to 2 tablespoons is also an option but the taste will be slightly milder.

• For those on restricted diets, substitute margarine or olive oil for butter when sautéing. The cream can be omitted from the sauce but this may require an additional amount of demi-glaze.

• Chanterelles are only in season for a short time. Shiitakes or other wild mushrooms make good substitutes.

RICHARD BILLINGHAM

ROASTED RACK OF LAMB
WITH GREEN PEPPERCORN SOUFFLÉ

Rack of Lamb
2 8-bone racks of lamb, trimmed and frenched
2 tablespoons green peppercorns
2 tablespoons chopped parsley
2 tablespoons Dijon mustard
2 egg whites
½ cup bread crumbs

Sauce
½ cup red wine
1 tablespoon butter

PREPARATION

1. Rack of Lamb. Preheat oven to 400 degrees. Place lamb in roasting pan and cook until rare, approximately 30–40 minutes. Crush peppercorns and mix with parsley and mustard. Whisk egg whites until stiff and fold in peppercorn mixture. Remove lamb from pan and set aside for 5 minutes.

After lamb has rested, coat meat side with ¼ inch of peppercorn mixture. Sprinkle with bread crumbs and return lamb to pan. Place under broiler for 5 minutes or until golden. Remove from pan and set on platter or cutting board.

2. Sauce. Discard fat from roasting pan and add wine, stirring until well mixed. Strain sauce and return to pan. Continue cooking until slightly reduced, then stir in butter.

3. Serving. Carve racks and place 3–4 ribs on each plate. Top with sauce.

NOTE

• Sauce can also be made by using margarine instead of butter or by omitting the butter entirely for those on restricted diets.

SERVES: 4
PREPARATION: 10 minutes
COOKING: 30–40 minutes

AUGUSTA

Augusta
The Westin Hotel
Tabor Center
1672 Lawrence Street
Denver, Colorado 80202
(303) 572-7222

In the heart of downtown Denver, Augusta is the Westin Tabor Center's four-diamond dining room. Set against the backdrop of the city's spectacular skyline, Augusta offers the finest of American cuisine prepared in classic European method by Executive Chef Roland Ulber.

ROLAND ULBER

ROASTED RACK OF LAMB HERB DE PROVENÇE

2 tablespoons finely chopped assorted fresh herbs
    (rosemary, thyme, parsley, and oregano)

¼ cup olive oil

2 8-boned racks of lamb, trimmed and frenched

Salt and pepper to taste

½ teaspoon Coleman's dry mustard

1 teaspoon water

2 tablespoons Dijon mustard

1 cup bread crumbs

1 clove garlic, minced

1 cup mint jelly

PREPARATION

Preheat oven to 425 degrees. Place herbs in bowl and add oil, stirring to form a pesto. Cut both racks in half, allowing 3–4 bones per person. Season with salt and pepper. Heat large sauté pan, add lamb, and sear only until browned; do not cook meat. Set aside to cool.

Combine dry mustard with water, then mix with Dijon, and spread over lamb. In pie plate mix bread crumbs, garlic, and herb pesto. Pat bread crumb mixture onto lamb, place lamb upright in roasting pan, and bake 15 minutes for rare, 25 minutes for medium. Slice lamb between bones, arrange meat on plates, drizzle with pan drippings, and spoon mint jelly near lamb.

SERVES: 4
PREPARATION: 10–15 minutes
COOKING: 15–25 minutes

THE BROADMOOR

The Penrose Room
The Broadmoor
One Lake Avenue
Colorado Springs, Colorado 80906
(719) 634-7711

A grand resort hotel built in 1918, The Broadmoor reflects a legacy of elegance, impeccable service, and exquisite dining. The Penrose Room serves continental cuisine, prepared at tableside, and is truly worthy of its Mobil five-star and AAA five-diamond ratings.

SIEGFRIED EISENBERGER

Texas Axis Venison with Spicy Blackberry Pepper Sauce

Spicy Blackberry Pepper Sauce

1 tablespoon olive oil

1 rib celery, diced

½ onion, diced

½ carrot, diced

2 serrano chilies

1 tablespoon chopped fresh herbs
(sage, rosemary, thyme)

1 tablespoon tomato paste

1 cup good quality red wine

3 cups veal stock

1 pint fresh blackberries, puréed;
reserve 8 whole berries for garnish

2 tablespoons pickled green peppercorns

Salt and pepper to taste

Texas Axis Venison

4 5-ounce venison loins,
cleaned and defatted *(see Notes)*

SERVES: 4

PREPARATION: 10 minutes

COOKING: 1 hour, 10 minutes

Zenith American Grill
1735 Arapahoe Street
Denver, Colorado 80202
(303) 820-2800

Zenith American Grill is home to a new class of western cooking. Chef Kevin Taylor uses regional ingredients and organic vegetables when creating dishes with Asian, Italian, or Southwestern influences. Each plate is a piece of art, presented like a de Kooning canvas.

Preparation

1. Spicy Blackberry Pepper Sauce. Heat oil in sauté pan and sauté vegetables, chilies, and herbs until dark brown in color. Stir in tomato paste and continue cooking until tomato paste caramelizes (dark brown). Add wine, stirring until mixed, and cook until syrupy. Add stock and cook until reduced to 1½ cups. Pour through fine-mesh strainer, then add blackberry purée and green peppercorns. Season with salt and pepper. (Recipe may be made to this point, 1 day in advance, and reheated.)

2. Texas Axis Venison. Cook venison on charcoal grill or sauté until medium-rare. Let meat rest 2–5 minutes before slicing.

3. Serving. Fan meat on each plate, cover with ¼–⅓ cup sauce, and garnish with blackberries.

Notes

• Steamed vegetables and fried sweet potatoes complement this dish.

• Buffalo, antelope, and boar meat are good substitutes for the venison. If your local butcher can not supply these meats you can call Game Sales International (800-729-2090). They ship, overnight, throughout the United States.

• Veal stock can be purchased from many local restaurants if you don't have time to make your own.

• Jalapeño chilies can be substituted for the serranos, but use only 1½ jalapeños.

• Frozen blackberries can be substituted for fresh.

KEVIN TAYLOR

RACK OF LAMB WITH APRICOT-ROSEMARY SAUCE, WILD RICE AND CASHEWS, STEAMED ASPARAGUS AND PIMENTO BUTTER

SERVES: 2–3
PREPARATION: 30 minutes
COOKING: 1 hour

C Lazy U Ranch

C Lazy U Ranch
P.O. Box 379
Granby, Colorado 80446
(970) 887-3344

C Lazy U Ranch, one of the country's outstanding guest ranches, has received both Mobil's five-star and AAA's five-diamond awards for the past thirteen years. Guests dine overlooking a breath-taking expanse of mountains and meadows. Summer or winter, C Lazy U Ranch is an experience of a lifetime.

STEPHEN REYNOLDS

Rack of Lamb
1 8-bone rack of lamb, trimmed and frenched

Salt and pepper

Wild Rice and Cashews
1 cup long-grain wild rice

1 cup apple juice

¼ cup apple liqueur

1 tablespoon butter or canola oil

½ cup roughly chopped cashews

½ medium red Delicious apple, cored and diced

1 cup fresh spinach, julienned

Salt and pepper to taste

Apricot-Rosemary Sauce
Lamb trimmings

1 tablespoon all-purpose flour

½ cup apricot brandy

½ cup apricot preserves

1 clove garlic, chopped

1 lemon, juice and zest

2 sprigs fresh rosemary

Pimento Butter
½ cup Marsala wine

1 medium shallot, chopped

½ cup chopped pimentos

4 tablespoons unsalted butter, cubed

Sugar, salt, and pepper to taste

Steamed Asparagus
1 bunch fresh asparagus

PREPARATION

1. Rack of Lamb. Preheat oven to 375 degrees. Heat ovenproof skillet until hot. Season lamb with salt and pepper and sear until browned on both sides and ends. Pour off excess fat and place lamb, meat side up, in skillet. Roast in oven for 30–45 minutes, depending on cooking preference. Place lamb on cutting board, let sit 10 minutes, then carve lamb between bones.

2. Wild Rice with Apples and Cashews. Bring 8 cups water to a rapid boil, stir in rice, reduce heat, and cook covered until tender, approximately 35–45 minutes. In saucepan, cook apple juice and apple liqueur until reduced to ¼ cup. When rice is cooked, drain excess liquid and set rice aside. Return pan to burner and heat oil. Add cashews and apples and sauté until browned. Return rice to pan, add reduced apple juice mixture and spinach, and season with salt and pepper.

3. Apricot-Rosemary Sauce. In saucepan, cook lamb trimmings until fat is rendered. Pour off excess fat, add flour to browned scraps, and cook, stirring until flour is browned. Add water to cover and simmer 20 minutes. Strain lamb trimmings and return liquid to saucepan. Add brandy, preserves, garlic, lemon juice, and rosemary, and cook until thickens to sauce consistency.

4. Pimento Butter. Put Marsala and shallots in saucepan and cook over medium-low heat until reduced by half. Add pimentos, reduce heat to low, and whisk in butter 1 piece at a time, until melted. Season with sugar, salt, and pepper.

5. Steamed Asparagus. Remove and discard tough part of stems and steam asparagus until just tender and bright green.

6. Serving. Place sliced rack on plate so bones fan in 1 direction and top with apricot-rosemary sauce. Spoon wild rice next to rack. Place asparagus opposite rack and top with pimento butter.

Parry primrose, Rocky Mountain National Park

VEAL MIGNON WITH GINGER-LEMON SAUCE AND BROCCOLI MOUSSELINE

SERVES: 4
PREPARATION: 20 minutes
COOKING: 15 minutes

Picasso

Picasso
The Lodge at Cordillera
2205 Cordillera Way
Edwards, Colorado 81632
(970) 926-2200

Located on top of a mountain with spectacular views of New York Mountain and the Vail Valley, Picasso's is European elegance with Rocky Mountain scenery. Its award-winning contemporary French cuisine and outstanding wine list make any occasion here special.

FABRICE BEAUDOIN

Ginger-Lemon Sauce
1 lemon
1 medium gingerroot, about thumb size
1 cup water
3 tablespoons sugar
1 tablespoon honey
1 tablespoon red wine vinegar
1 cup orange juice
2 tablespoons butter

Broccoli Mousseline
2 heads broccoli
2 tablespoons olive oil
Salt and pepper to taste

Veal
1–2 tablespoons butter or olive oil
4 6-ounce veal tenderloins
Salt and pepper to taste

Garnish
1 lemon, sliced

PREPARATION

1. Ginger-Lemon Sauce. Peel lemon and julienne rind. Peel gingerroot and julienne. Blanch lemon and gingerroot in separate pans of boiling water for 1–2 minutes. Drain and blanch once more. Place lemon and gingerroot in saucepan, add 1 cup water and sugar, and cook until tender. Remove gingerroot and reserve; discard water and lemon. Return ginger to saucepan, add honey and vinegar, and cook until reduced to 1 teaspoon. Add orange juice and reduce to ¼ cup. Whisk in butter, transfer to blender or food processor, and purée 1 minute. Strain and keep warm.

2. Broccoli Mousseline. Cook broccoli in lightly salted water until tender; drain. Purée broccoli and oil in blender or food processor. Keep warm.

3. Veal. In sauté pan, heat butter or oil and sauté veal until medium-rare. Season with salt and pepper.

4. Serving. Place 2 tablespoons broccoli mousseline on each plate, lay veal next to broccoli, pour sauce over veal, and garnish with lemon slices.

NOTE

• For those on restricted diets, substitute margarine for butter in the ginger sauce, or omit the butter entirely, which will give the sauce a slightly stronger flavor.

GRILLED PORK TENDERLOIN
WITH APPLE BRANDY MUSTARD SAUCE

Veal Stock
5 pounds veal bones
1 bunch celery, without leaves
10 large yellow onions
8 large carrots
10 very ripe tomatoes
15 black peppercorns
4 bay leaves
2 gallons tomato juice
   (preferably fresh)

Apple Brandy Mustard Sauce
1½ cups brandy
2 Granny Smith apples, peeled,
   cored, and finely chopped
1 bay leaf
6 black peppercorns
⅔ cup honey
1½ cups veal stock
1½ cups whipping cream,
   warmed slightly to prevent curdling
¼ cup whole-grain mustard

Pork Tenderloin
3 pounds pork tenderloin
Peanut oil
Salt and pepper

SERVES: 6
PREPARATION: 30 minutes
(veal stock requires 72 hours, *see Notes*)
COOKING: 30 minutes

CACHE
CACHE

Cache Cache
205 South Mill Street
Aspen, Colorado 81611
(970) 925-3835

Cache Cache is an innovative
French Bistro serving the food
of Provence. In a warm, cozy
atmosphere filled with fresh
flowers and objets d'art, patrons
enjoy healthy foods prepared
without fats or butter.

PREPARATION

1. Veal Stock. Stock should be made at least 72 hours prior to serving. Roast bones in pan at 300 degrees until browned, then place bones in 3–5-gallon stockpot. Roughly cut vegetables, leaving skins on. Roast vegetables in same pan until soft and transfer to stockpot. Add peppercorns and bay leaves.

The size of the stockpot will determine how much tomato juice to add initially. The tomato juice should comprise half to two thirds of total liquid. The remaining amount should be cold water. Fill pot with liquid, but not so much that it will spill over when heated. Cook uncovered over very low heat for 72 hours. As separation takes place, add remaining tomato juice or cold water. Skim grease from top, especially during first 24 hours or stock will become bitter.

After 72 hours, pour through very fine mesh strainer or cheesecloth. Return to pot and cook over medium-high heat. Place pot slightly off center on burner, allowing impurities to collect on side for easy extraction. Cook until liquid is reduced by two thirds. The end product should be a sweet, rich, brown glaze.

2. Apple Brandy Mustard Sauce. In saucepan combine brandy, apples, bay leaf, peppercorns, and honey. Bring to a boil, reduce heat to low, and simmer until reduced by one third. Add veal stock and reduce by one third. Add whipping cream and mustard and reduce by one third again. Remove bay leaf and purée thoroughly.

3. Pork Tenderloin. Lightly brush pork with peanut oil, season with salt and pepper, and grill slowly until medium-rare to medium. Slice tenderloin.

4. Serving. Cover plates with sauce and place tenderloin slices in center of each plate.

NOTES

   • Veal stock may be purchased from many local restaurants if you do not have the time to make your own.

   • Veal stock can be frozen for future use.

MICHAEL W. BEARY

VEAL LOIN LADEN WITH APRICOTS AND WILD MUSHROOMS

SERVES: 6
PREPARATION: 20 minutes
COOKING: 1 hour

Flagstaff House

Flagstaff House
1138 Flagstaff Road
Boulder, Colorado 80302
(303) 442-4640

Flagstaff House, built in 1929 as a mountain cabin overlooking Boulder, is a Mobil *four-star,* AAA *four-diamond, and* The Wine Spectator's *grand award-winning restaurant. Owned and operated by Don Monette and his sons Mark and Scott, Flagstaff House is renowned for its innovative dishes and extensive wine cellar.*

Veal
2 teaspoons olive oil
1 pound shiitake mushrooms, sliced
2 cloves garlic, minced
2 shallots, minced
2 tablespoons unsalted butter
4 ounces dried apricots, sliced
1 teaspoon each chopped fresh,
    thyme, sage, rosemary, and oregano
2½ pounds veal loin, with pocket

Sauce
6 ounces dried apricots
¼ cup brandy
Olive oil
6 shallots, sliced
4 cups veal stock
2 tablespoons butter

PREPARATION

1. Veal. Preheat oven to 325 degrees. In large sauté pan, heat oil. Add mushrooms, garlic, and shallots and sauté until tender. Stir in butter, apricots, and herbs. Remove from heat and cool. When cooled, stuff veal and tie roast (*see Notes*). Bake until meat reaches 170 degrees, about 45 minutes.

2. Sauce. Soak apricots in brandy for 15 minutes, then chop. In medium pan, heat small amount of oil and cook shallots over medium-low heat until translucent. Add apricots and brandy and reduce to a glaze. Add veal stock and reduce by half. Whisk in butter.

3. Serving. Slice veal, place on individual plates, and top with sauce.

NOTES

• Ask your butcher to cut a pocket in the veal loin and to tie the roast loosely so you can retie the loin once it is stuffed.

• Veal stock may be purchased from many local restaurants.

MARK MONETTE

Sunset over Mount Nystrom, Vasquez Peak Wilderness

ANAHEIM FILET WITH ANCHO CHILI BUTTER

SERVES: 6

PREPARATION: 15 minutes

COOKING: 15–20 minutes

Ancho Chili Butter

1 pound unsalted butter, softened

3 tablespoons puréed ancho chili *(see Note)*

1 cup crumbled Gorgonzola cheese

Steaks

6 8-ounce tenderloin steaks

6 whole Anaheim chilies,
    roasted and peeled *(see Note)*

Salt and pepper to taste

PREPARATION

1. Ancho Chili Butter. Combine all ingredients and keep at room temperature until ready to use.

2. Steaks. Make 1-inch cut in the side of each steak, then carefully run knife inside, making a pocket for the chili. Stuff 1 chili in each steak and grill until medium-rare, approximately 8 minutes on both sides.

3. Serving. Top each steak with ancho butter and serve immediately.

NOTE

• Ancho chilies are most commonly sold dried. They are reconstituted in hot water, then puréed and passed through a sieve or fine-mesh strainer. Roasted, peeled Anaheim chilies are available in a can. For fresh chilies, either Anaheim or ancho, roast on grill or under broiler until skins are charred, remove from heat, peel, and seed.

THE BRISTOL
AT ARROWHEAD

The Bristol at Arrowhead
Country Club of the Rockies
676 Sawatch Drive
Edwards, Colorado 81632
(970) 926-2111

*Nationally acclaimed,
The Bristol at Arrowhead is
located in the Country Club
of the Rockies and is open
to the public for fine dining.
Featuring creative American
cuisine, gracious service, and a
magnificent setting, The Bristol
offers something for everyone.*

DENNIS B. CORWIN

Eagle River, near Edwards

BRAISED VEAL CHOP WITH SWEET PEAS AND MINT

Olive oil for sautéing
6 10-ounce veal rib chops
9 small red potatoes, quartered
18 baby carrots, sliced
3 shallots, diced
1 pound mushrooms, sliced
2 tablespoons all-purpose flour
½ cup red wine
1 15-ounce can reduced-salt beef broth
2 bunches fresh mint, chopped
2 cups frozen sweet peas
4 tablespoons butter
Salt and pepper to taste

PREPARATION

Preheat oven to 325 degrees. In large skillet, heat oil, brown veal chops, and place in large roasting pan. In same skillet, add potatoes and carrots and cook until carrots begin to soften and potatoes brown. Transfer to roasting pan.

Add shallots to skillet and cook until translucent, then add mushrooms and cook until browned. Stir in flour and cook 1 minute. Add red wine and cook 5 minutes. Stir in beef broth and half of mint and pour into roasting pan. Bake covered for 20 minutes.

Arrange potatoes, carrots, and veal chops on plates. Place roasting pan on burner, stir in peas and butter, and cook 2 minutes. Spoon sauce over veal and garnish with remaining mint.

SERVES: 6
PREPARATION: 10 minutes
COOKING: 50 minutes

Beano's Cabin
Beaver Creek Resort
P.O. Box 915
Avon, Colorado 81620
(970) 949-9090

Beano's Cabin, situated high above the Beaver Creek resort, is the perfect mountaintop dining experience. Depending on the season, you arrive here via a snowcat-drawn sleigh, horse-drawn wagon, van, or on even horseback. You are then treated to an exceptional six-course prix fixe dinner.

JOSEPH P. KEEGAN

ROASTED RACK OF COLORADO LAMB VERMONT STYLE, WITH MAPLE SYRUP GLAZE AND MARSALA CIDER SAUCE

SERVES: 6
PREPARATION: 15 minutes
COOKING: 40–50 minutes

krabloonik

Krabloonik
4250 Divide Road
Snowmass Village, Colorado 81615
(970) 923-4342

At Krabloonik, home to the
world's largest husky kennel,
guests can tour the kennels or
experience the thrill of a dog
sled ride before dining on wild
game specialties. A log cabin with
sunken fire pit, the Krabloonik
provides a relaxed, elegant location
for a true Colorado experience.

Marsala Cider Sauce
1¾ cups Marsala wine
½ cup white wine
¾ cup apple cider
1 shallot, diced
1 tablespoon honey
1 teaspoon cider vinegar

Roasted Rack of Colorado Lamb
3 8-boned racks of lamb, trimmed and frenched
2 cups pure Vermont maple syrup
1 teaspoon each salt and pepper

PREPARATION

1. Marsala Cider Sauce. Pour wines into large saucepan, bring to a boil, and ignite by touching a match to the side of the pan (be very careful, for flames can be high). When flame burns out, add cider, shallots, honey, and vinegar. Cook until liquid is reduced to 1½ cups.

2. Roasted Rack of Colorado Lamb. Preheat oven to 400 degrees. Salt and pepper fat cap side of lamb, place in roasting pan, and bake for 15 minutes. Once a nice seared cap is attained, turn rack over and cover with maple syrup. Reduce heat to 325 degrees and bake until medium-rare, continuing to baste lamb with syrup in roasting pan.

Remove lamb from oven and brush with syrup in pan, allowing a candy coating to form. Return lamb to oven for 5 minutes prior to serving. Slice into chops.

3. Serving. Spoon sauce around plate and arrange lamb in center.

JOHN ROBERTS

Spring aspen grove, Gunnison National Forest

CAPELLINI POMODORO

Marinara Sauce
½ cup olive oil
½ cup finely chopped celery
1 cup finely chopped onions
½ cup finely chopped carrots
2 tablespoons puréed garlic
1½ 1-pound cans stewed plum tomatoes
1 cup chicken stock
1 tablespoon fennel seed
1 tablespoon dried thyme
1 tablespoon dried basil
1 tablespoon dried oregano
1½ tablespoons honey
Salt and pepper to taste

Pomodoro Sauce
¼ cup extra-virgin olive oil
10 cloves garlic, thinly sliced
16 ripe tomatoes, cored, seeded,
    and cut into bite-sized pieces
⅓ cup chicken stock
⅔ cup marinara sauce
½ cup coarsely chopped fresh basil
Salt and pepper to taste

Capellini
1 1-pound box Di Cecco capellini

Garnish
Sprig of fresh basil

SERVES: 6
PREPARATION: 15 minutes
COOKING: 15 minutes *(see Notes)*

traMonti
The Charter at Beaver Creek
120 Offerson Road
Beaver Creek, Colorado 81620
(970) 949-5552

*traMonti, one of the Vail Valley's
finest restaurants, features both
traditional and contemporary
Italian cuisine. With spectacular
views of Beaver Creek Mountain
and a warm inviting atmosphere,
traMonti is a favorite of visitors
and locals alike.*

PREPARATION

1. Marinara Sauce. In large sauté pan, heat oil and sauté celery, onions, and carrots until tender; add garlic. Purée tomatoes and add to pan along with remaining ingredients. Simmer uncovered over low heat for 1½ hours.

2. Pomodoro Sauce. In large pan, heat oil, add garlic, and cook for 30 seconds. Add tomatoes and cook 1 minute. Add chicken stock, marinara sauce, and basil, and cook 4 minutes. (Tomatoes should not be overcooked; they should keep their shape.) Season with salt and pepper.

3. Capellini. Cook capellini according to package instructions.

4. Serving. Pour pomodoro sauce over capellini and garnish with a fresh basil.

NOTE

• The recipe calls for marinara sauce, which requires 1½ hours to cook. However, a good-quality marinara from a jar can be substituted for homemade. If you do make the marinara sauce from scratch, the amount left over can be frozen.

CYNDE ARNOLD

STEAMED WHOLE MAINE LOBSTER WITH ASPARAGUS AND PASSION FRUIT SAUCE OVER ANGEL HAIR PASTA

SERVES: 4

PREPARATION: 10 minutes

COOKING: 20 minutes

The Black Swan

The Black Swan
200 Inverness Drive West
Englewood, Colorado 80112
(303) 799-5800

The Black Swan, rated four-diamonds by AAA, offers exceptional international cuisine. Enjoy a relaxed yet elegant atmosphere where service is paramount. The Black Swan is perfect for an intimate rendezvous or a serious business dinner.

Passion Fruit Sauce
2 cups passion fruit juice
1 cup white wine
1 lime, juice only
½ pound butter, cut in pieces (optional)
Pinch of salt and white pepper

Lobster, Asparagus and Angel Hair Pasta
4 1½-pound lobsters
32 thin asparagus spears
1 1-pound box angel hair pasta

PREPARATION

1. Passion Fruit Sauce. In saucepan, add passion fruit juice, wine, and lime juice, and simmer until reduced by half. If using butter, slowly whisk in, 1 piece at a time. Season with salt and pepper.

2. Lobster, Asparagus and Angel Hair Pasta. Bring 3 pots of water to a boil (1 for lobster, 1 to steam asparagus, and 1 for pasta). Steam lobsters for 5–7 minutes, steam asparagus for about 5 minutes, and cook pasta according to package directions.

3. Serving. Remove lobster meat in whole pieces from tail and claws. Toss pasta with sauce and place in center of each plate. Place meat on pasta so it resembles a lobster body and arrange asparagus to mimic lobster legs.

NOTE

• Passion fruit juice can be found in the frozen juice section of most grocery stores. A blend of tropical juices can also be used.

NIELS VAN LEEUWEN

FREDERICK CLABAUGH

WILD MUSHROOMS AND LOBSTER RISOTTO

½ cup dry mushroom mix
4½ cups boiling water, divided
3 cups chicken stock
¼ pound butter
½ cup finely diced yellow onion
2 teaspoons puréed garlic
1 cup sliced shiitake mushrooms
3 cups arborio rice
1 cup white wine
1 cup coarsely chopped lobster meat
½ cup grated Parmesan cheese
½ cup finely diced tomatoes
2 tablespoons chopped fresh parsley
Salt and pepper to taste

SERVES: 6
PREPARATION: 20 minutes
COOKING: 35 minutes

traMonti
The Charter at Beaver Creek
120 Offerson Road
Beaver Creek, Colorado 81620
(970) 949-5552

traMonti, one of the Vail Valley's finest restaurants, features both traditional and contemporary Italian cuisine. With spectacular views of Beaver Creek Mountain and a warm inviting atmosphere, traMonti is a favorite of visitors and locals alike.

PREPARATION

Soak dry mushrooms in 2½ cups of the boiling water until soft, approximately 10 minutes. Remove mushrooms, chop, and set aside. Strain liquid through cheesecloth or coffee filter to remove grit and reserve 2 cups. Combine chicken stock and reserved mushroom liquid in saucepan, bring to a boil, and simmer.

Melt butter in stockpot or large saucepan and add onions, garlic, shiitake mushrooms, and rehydrated mushrooms. Sauté until onions are soft, approximately 3 minutes. Add arborio rice, stirring until rice is completely coated with butter. Add wine, stirring until absorbed. Add 2 cups of the chicken stock-and-mushroom mixture, stirring until absorbed. Add remaining 2 cups boiling water, stirring until absorbed. Repeat until all liquid is absorbed and risotto is cooked. It will have a creamy consistency.

Stir in lobster, Parmesan cheese, tomatoes, and parsley. Season with salt and pepper and serve immediately.

NOTE

• Risotto is made from an Italian short-grain rice with a large starch coat. When cooked slowly, it releases the starch and combines with the stock to create a creamy, rich sauce. It is very important to: (1) coat the rice with butter before adding any liquid; (2) heat the liquid first and add in small amounts, just enough to cover the rice and allow it to be absorbed before adding more liquid; and (3) continuously stir the risotto.

CYNDE ARNOLD

PRAWNS IN A TOMATO-FENNEL BROTH OVER LINGUINE

Tomato-Fennel Broth
2 tablespoons extra-virgin olive oil
2 teaspoons chopped shallots
2 tablespoons chopped garlic
1 bulb fennel, chopped
¼ cup firmly packed fresh basil
1 carrot, chopped
1 leek, chopped
1 cup white wine
1 teaspoon saffron
2 cups fish stock
1 bay leaf
1½ teaspoons minced fresh oregano
1 teaspoon salt
1 box Pomi tomatoes, chopped *(see Note)*

Prawns and Linguine
1 pound prawns (jumbo shrimp)
½ teaspoon each cayenne pepper,
  black pepper, and minced garlic
1 tablespoon olive oil
1 1-pound box linguine

Garnish
1 carrot, julienned
Fennel leaves

SERVES: 4
PREPARATION: 30 minutes
COOKING: 1 hour

The Bristol at Arrowhead
Country Club of the Rockies
676 Sawatch Drive
Edwards, Colorado 81632
(970) 926-2111

*Nationally acclaimed, The
Bristol at Arrowhead is located
in the Country Club of the
Rockies and is open to the
public for fine dining.
Featuring creative American
cuisine, gracious service, and
a magnificent setting, The
Bristol offers something for
everyone.*

PREPARATION

1. Tomato-Fennel Broth. In small pan heat oil and sauté shallots and garlic. Transfer to stockpot, add remaining ingredients, except for the salt and one forth of the tomatoes. Simmer 1 hour, strain, and return liquid to stockpot. Add salt and remaining tomatoes and bring to a boil. Remove from heat and strain, pressing mixture with spoon to extract as much liquid as possible.

2. Prawns and Linguine. While broth is simmering, prepare prawns and pasta. Peel, devein, and butterfly the prawns. Mix cayenne, black pepper, garlic, and oil in bowl, add prawns and marinate 5 minutes. Grill until pink. Prepare linguine according to package directions.

3. Serving. Place equal portions of linguine in bowls and toss with about ½ cup broth. (The linguine will turn yellow from the saffron.) Arrange 3 prawns on top, add additional broth if desired, and serve immediately.

NOTE

• Pomi tomatoes come in a box and can be found in health food stores, specialty stores, and selected grocery stores.

DENNIS B. CORWIN

Veal Steak Flambé over Fettuccine

Fettuccine
1   1-pound box fettuccine

Veal Steak
12 small veal mignon steaks
Paprika
Salt and white pepper
2 tablespoons butter
2 tablespoons cognac

Sauce
½ cup demi-glaze
Pinch of curry powder
2 tablespoons heavy cream

SERVES: 4
PREPARATION: 5 minutes
COOKING: 10–15 minutes

The Black Bear Inn

The Black Bear Inn
42 East Main Street
Lyons, Colorado 80540
(303) 823-6812

Old World charm and a unique combination of food, wine, cocktails, and imported beers make dining at this Swiss-style restaurant an unforgettable experience. The restaurant, located on the east edge of Lyons, offers professional services for private parties, weddings, and receptions.

PREPARATION

1. Fettucine. Cook according to package instructions.

2. Veal Steak. Season veal well with paprika and salt and pepper. Melt butter in large skillet, add veal, and sauté until golden brown on both sides. Add cognac and ignite by touching a match to side of pan (be very careful, for flames can be high). Baste meat with burning liquid. Remove veal when flame burns out and keep warm. Return pan to stove.

3. Sauce. Add demi-glaze to veal skillet and simmer, stirring continuously. Sprinkle with curry powder and blend in cream.

4. Serving. Slice the veal. Place fettuccine on each plate, top with slices of veal, and drizzle with sauce.

NOTE

• Demi-glaze is a reduced meat stock that can be purchased from most local restaurants. If none is available, simmer 1½ cups unsalted beef broth until reduced to ½ cup.

HANS J. WYPPLER

SHRIMP SAMBUCA OVER PENNE PASTA

Penne Pasta
1   1-pound package penne pasta

Shrimp Sambuca
Olive oil for sautéing
12 jumbo shrimp, peeled and deveined
2 tablespoons chopped garlic
¼ cup diced roasted red bell peppers
¼ cup diced scallions
¼ cup Sambuca
¼ cup heavy cream
¼ pound cold butter, cut in pieces
Salt and pepper to taste

PREPARATION

1. Penne Pasta. Cook according to package directions.

2. Shrimp Sambuca. Heat a small amount of oil in large sauté pan and sauté shrimp until pink. Remove shrimp and keep warm. Add garlic, roasted peppers, and scallions, and sauté 1 minute. Add Sambuca, stirring to dissolve small particles in bottom of pan. Add cream and continue cooking until liquid is reduced by half. Whisk in cold butter, 1 piece at a time. Season with salt and pepper. Return shrimp to pan and cook 1 minute.

3. Serving. Divide pasta among the plates, spoon on shrimp and sauce, and serve immediately.

NOTE

• Heavy cream and butter can be replaced with milk and margarine or omitted entirely. If omitted, increase Sambuca to ⅓ cup, return shrimp to pan after adding Sambuca, and cook 1 minute.

SERVES: 4
PREPARATION: 10 minutes
COOKING: 10 minutes

TUSCANY

Tuscany
Loews Giorgio Hotel
4150 East Mississippi Avenue
Denver, Colorado 80222
(303) 782-9300

With fresh-cut flowers, marble fireplace, and an evening harpist, the Tuscany is the perfect setting for dining on exquisitely prepared Italian cuisine. The award-winning menu is complemented by a large selection of Italian wines. Tuscany is ideal for celebrating any occasion—or creating one.

TIM A. FIELDS

CHICKEN SAUSAGE PIZZA WITH
SWEET CORN, CHERRY TOMATOES AND GOAT CHEESE

SERVES: 6

PREPARATION: 30 minutes
(1 hour for rising)

COOKING: 8–10 minutes

Sweet Basil
193 East Gore Creek Drive
Vail, Colorado 81657
(970) 476-0125

Sweet Basil features imaginative American cuisine with Mediterranean and Asian influences. The menu, which changes frequently, remains true to each season. Sweet Basil's primary goal is to create food that excites the palate, is visually arresting, and leaves a lasting impression.

Dough

1 package dry yeast

¾ cup warm water

1 teaspoon salt

1 tablespoon honey

2 tablespoons olive oil

1 cup cold water

2½ cups all-purpose flour

Chicken Sausage

¾ pound chicken leg meat

⅓ pound pork shoulder, cubed

1 teaspoon chopped garlic

1 tablespoon grated Parmesan cheese

1 teaspoon salt

⅛ teaspoon pepper

Pinch of cumin

Pinch of coriander

1 teaspoon each chopped fresh basil, chives, and parsley

¼ cup unsalted chicken stock

Toppings

8 ounces mozzarella cheese

48 cherry tomatoes, halved

4 ears corn, kernels sliced from cob

2 tablespoons chopped fresh oregano

4 ounces goat cheese

PREPARATION

1. Dough. Dissolve yeast in warm water and let sit 10 minutes. Combine salt, honey, oil, and cold water in large bowl. Add yeast mixture, then flour. Knead until smooth and glossy. Divide into 8 equal portions and set aside in a warm place for 1 hour.

2. Chicken Sausage. Combine all ingredients, except chopped herbs and chicken stock, and place on baking sheet. Put in freezer for 40 minutes. Preheat oven to 500 degrees. Grind ingredients from freezer in food processor, add herbs and chicken stock, and continue mixing. Return to baking sheet and bake 5 minutes. Remove from oven and crumble.

3. Serving. Form each section of dough into small pizza rounds. Arrange chicken sausage and toppings on pizza dough and bake at 500 degrees until golden brown. (Optional: remove from oven, brush with olive oil and return to oven for 1 minute.) Serve.

THOMAS SALAMUNOVICH

Autumn aspen trees, Beaver Creek Wilderness Study Area

GRILLED PORTABELLO MUSHROOMS
WITH ARUGULA AND SAGE POLENTA

Sage Polenta

5⅓ cups water

1⅓ cups coarse cornmeal

⅔ bunch scallions, white part only

½ bell pepper, chopped

1⅓ tablespoons chopped fresh sage

2⅔ tablespoons pine nuts

2⅔ tablespoons chili oil

1 teaspoon kosher salt

Arugula with Sherry Vinaigrette

24 cloves garlic

¼ cup pine nuts

1 pound arugula

¼ cup sherry vinegar

⅓ cup olive oil

Grilled Portabello Mushrooms

16 portabello mushrooms, stemmed

½ cup olive oil

Salt and pepper

SERVES: 8

PREPARATION: 15 minutes
(polenta refrigerates overnight)

COOKING: 25 minutes

Terra Bistro
352 East Meadow Drive
Vail, Colorado 81657
(970) 476-6836

*Terra Bistro, located in the Vail
Athletic Club, takes a holistic
approach to dining, offering
sophisticated international
cuisine prepared with natural
ingredients and specializing
in free-range meats and
poultry. Food is prepared to
reduce fat content while
maintaining flavor.*

PREPARATION

1. Sage Polenta. In heavy-bottomed saucepan, bring water to a boil and slowly whisk in cornmeal. Reduce heat to medium and cook 5 minutes, stirring continuously. Add scallions and bell peppers and cook 15 minutes, stirring frequently. Stir in sage, pine nuts, chili oil, and salt. Pour into 12x24-inch baking pan lined with wax paper, smooth top, cover with wax paper, and refrigerate overnight. Right before serving, cut into squares. Lightly brush with oil and grill 5 minutes on each side. (Polenta can be grilled along with portabello mushrooms.)

2. Arugula with Sherry Vinaigrette. Preheat oven to 375 degrees. Place garlic on baking sheet and bake 15 minutes; set aside. Heat small skillet, add pine nuts, and cook over low heat until golden; set aside. Toss arugula with vinegar and oil.

3. Grilled Portabello Mushrooms. Lightly brush mushrooms with oil, then grill or broil 4–5 minutes on each side.

4. Serving. Place arugula on each plate, top with polenta, cover with portabellos, and garnish with garlic and pine nuts.

CYNTHIA WALT

GRILLED MARINATED VEGETABLES, CARAMELIZED CORN, SMOKY TOMATO VINAIGRETTE AND CHILI CORN BREAD

SERVES: 4

PREPARATION: 1 hour, 45 minutes
(see Notes)

COOKING: 1 hour, 10–15 minutes
(see Notes)

The Home Ranch
54880 Route 129
Clark, Colorado 80428
(970) 879-1780

Located at the northern end of the breathtaking Elk River Valley, The Home Ranch offers a gracious combination of western warmth, creature comforts, and lively outdoor activities. Rarely repeating a meal during the year has earned The Home Ranch both Mobil's four-star and AAA's four-diamond awards.

Clyde R. Nelson

CLYDE R. NELSON

Chili Corn Bread
¼ cup warm water
1 tablespoon yeast
¼ cup vegetable oil
¼ cup fresh or frozen corn kernels
2 eggs
1½ teaspoons salt
1½ teaspoons sugar
1½ teaspoons red pepper flakes
¼ pound Anaheim chilies,
   roasted, peeled, seeded and diced
Pinch of chili powder
½ teaspoon baking powder
¾ cup heavy cream
½ cup cornmeal
4¼ cups all-purpose flour
All-purpose flour for dusting

Smoky Tomato Vinaigrette
3–4 Roma tomatoes
2 tablespoons chopped mixed herbs
   (basil, thyme, marjoram, tarragon,
   and fennel)
2 tablespoons lemon juice or vinegar
1 large shallot, peeled and
   roughly chopped
½ cup extra-virgin olive oil

Basil Oil Marinade
1 cup extra-virgin olive oil
1 tablespoon chopped shallots
1½ teaspoons chopped garlic
1 tablespoon chopped fresh basil
1 tablespoon chopped fresh parsley
¾ teaspoon freshly ground black pepper
2 fresh sage leaves
1 tablespoon lemon juice
1½ teaspoons grated Parmesan cheese
1½ teaspoons pine nuts
¾ teaspoon salt

Caramelized Corn
1 tablespoon corn oil
4 ears corn, kernels cut from cob
2 tablespoons balsamic vinegar
Salt and pepper to taste

Grilled Vegetables
2 Japanese eggplants, halved lengthwise
2 zucchini, halved lengthwise
2 yellow summer squash,
   halved lengthwise
2 red bell peppers, seeded and
   cut in thirds
2 yellow bell peppers, seeded and
   cut in thirds
1 small jicama, peeled and
   cut in ¼-inch slices
2 portabello mushrooms
1 bunch green onions, sliced
8 spears asparagus, trimmed

PREPARATION

1. Chili Corn Bread. Combine water, yeast, oil, and corn in large bowl and mix thoroughly. Let stand until foamy. Add remaining ingredients and mix well to form a smooth dough. On lightly floured board, knead until smooth. Form dough into ball and place in lightly oiled bowl. Cover and let stand until doubled. Transfer to floured board, punch down, and shape into a loaf. Place on greased 9x5-inch pan and let rise. Bake at 350 degrees until bread has a solid crust and begins to turn golden, about 1 hour.

2. Smoky Tomato Vinaigrette. Grill or smoke tomatoes until skins begin to shrivel and remove from heat. Peel and discard skin, cut tomatoes in half, and squeeze out seeds. Dice pulp and place in sieve to drain. Combine with remaining ingredients.

3. Basil Oil Marinade. Purée all ingredients in a blender or food processor.

4. Caramelized Corn. Heat skillet over medium-high heat, add oil, and stir in corn. Cook, stirring, until kernels begin to brown and some pop. Place in mixing bowl, toss with balsamic vinegar and salt and pepper. Keep warm.

5. Grilled Marinated Vegetables. Place vegetables on wire rack, set on baking sheet, pour marinade over vegetables, and let excess drip off (or vegetables could burn). Grill over low heat, basting occasionally.

6. Serving. Cut portabello mushrooms in half. Arrange grilled vegetables around plates, drizzle with tomato vinaigrette, place corn in center, and accompany with corn bread.

NOTES

- Basil oil can be served with fresh breads for dipping.
- As with most breads, the chili corn bread requires time, about 1 hour 30 minutes to prepare and 1 hour to bake.

Bear Creek, Maroon Bells-Snowmass Wilderness

GOAT CHEESE STUFFED CHILIES WITH BLACK BEAN PURÉE

SERVES: 6 as an entrée
12 as an appetizer
PREPARATION: 30 minutes
COOKING: 2–2½ hours

La Petite Maison
1015 West Colorado Avenue
Colorado Springs, Colorado 80904
(719) 632-4887

Located in an old Victorian home, La Petite Maison is a small, intimate restaurant where the cuisine is a tender balance of classic cooking and innovative creation. The wine list is as outstanding as the cuisine.

Black Bean Purée
3 celery tops, chopped
½ carrot, chopped
½ pound black beans
½ small yellow onion, chopped
2 cloves garlic, chopped
4 cups unsalted chicken stock
¾ teaspoon ground cumin
¼ teaspoon cayenne pepper
½ teaspoon salt

Salsa
1 16-ounce can tomato sauce
3 green chilies, chopped
½ lime, juice only
1½ teaspoons chopped fresh basil
1 clove garlic, minced
½ teaspoon ground cumin
½ red onion, chopped
3 tomatoes, skinned, seeded, and chopped
Pinch of salt
Pinch of cayenne pepper
Dash of Worcestershire sauce

Chilies
12 whole Anaheim chilies
2½ tablespoons chopped fresh basil
8 ounces goat cheese, room temperature

PREPARATION

1. Black Bean Purée. In large saucepan, mix all ingredients, except cumin, cayenne, and salt; cover with water and simmer until beans are soft. (Beans should cook for 2–2½ hours.) If needed, add additional water. Stir in cumin and cayenne, then purée in small batches in blender or food processor. Season with salt.

2. Salsa. Mix all ingredients in a medium bowl.

3. Chilies. Roast, peel, and seed chilies. (Roasting can be done on grill or under broiler.) Press basil into goat cheese with fork. Using a pastry bag, pipe goat cheese mixture into center of chilies. If pastry bag is not available, use spoon.

4. Serving. Cover two 8-inch pie plates with black bean purée, place stuffed chilies on top, and spoon 2 tablespoons salsa over middle of each chili. Broil 90 seconds, making sure purée does not brown. Serve immediately.

HOLLY B. MERVIS

CREAMED CORN AND CILANTRO

1 teaspoon butter

2 teaspoons shallots

⅓ jalapeño pepper, seeded and chopped

1 poblano pepper, peeled and diced

1 teaspoon minced garlic

½ cup white wine

2½ cups heavy cream

¾ cup corn

¼ bunch fresh chopped cilantro

Salt and pepper to taste

PREPARATION

In medium saucepan, melt butter, and sauté shallots, jalapeños, poblanos, and garlic until soft. Add wine and continue cooking until reduced by half. Add remaining ingredients and cook until thickened. If needed, mix 1 teaspoon all-purpose flour with 1 tablespoon water and stir into mixture to thicken. Serve immediately.

NOTE

• This is actually a side dish and is wonderful as an accompaniment to grilled fowl and meat or served with Southwestern dishes such as Smoked Chicken and Wild Mushroom Burrito (page 89).

SERVES: 6
PREPARATION: 15 minutes
COOKING: 15 minutes

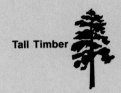

Tall Timber

Tall Timber
Box 90
Silverton Star Route
Durango, Colorado 81301
(970) 259-4813

Tall Timber, located in a wilderness setting in the heart of the San Juan Mountains, pampers its guests with five-star and five-diamond service. No roads lead to this luxury retreat; all guests arrive by either narrow-gauge railroad or helicopter to enjoy international cuisine and a variety of indoor and outdoor activities.

DENNIS J. SHAKAN

SEASONAL WILD MUSHROOMS AND ASPARAGUS TART

SERVES: 4 as an entrée
PREPARATION: 10–15 minutes
COOKING: 25–30 minutes

THE BROADMOOR

The Penrose Room
The Broadmoor
One Lake Avenue
Colorado Springs, Colorado 80906
(719) 634-7711

A grand resort hotel built in 1918,
The Broadmoor reflects a legacy
of elegance, impeccable service,
and exquisite dining. The Penrose
Room offers continental cuisine,
prepared at tableside, and is truly
worthy of its Mobil five-star and
AAA five-diamond ratings.

Asparagus Tart
6 stalks asparagus
1 tablespoon butter
1½ teaspoons minced shallots
12 ounces chopped wild mushrooms
½ cup white wine
½ cup heavy cream
Salt and pepper to taste
1 teaspoon chopped fresh parsley
4 4- to 5-inch tart shells *(see Notes)*

Marsala Sauce
1 tablespoon minced shallots
1 sprig fresh thyme
1 bay leaf
6 cracked peppercorns
½ cup burgundy wine
½ cup Marsala wine
1 cup demi-glaze *(see Notes)*
Salt and pepper to taste
1 tablespoon unsalted butter

PREPARATION

1. Asparagus Tart. Preheat oven to 350 degrees. Remove asparagus tips and set aside. Chop asparagus stems. Heat butter in sauté pan, add shallots, and cook over medium to medium-low heat until translucent. Add mushrooms and chopped asparagus and cook until all moisture has evaporated. Add wine, stirring to dissolve browned particles in bottom of pan; cook until liquid is reduced by three fourths. Add cream and cook until thickened. Season with salt and pepper and stir in parsley. Fill tart shells with mushroom mixture, place on baking sheets, and bake until shells are browned and centers are warm, approximately 20–25 minutes.

2. Marsala Sauce. Combine shallots, thyme, bay leaf, peppercorns, and burgundy in saucepan and bring a to boil. Reduce heat to medium and cook until reduced to ¼ cup. Add Marsala and cook until reduced to ¼ cup. Stir in demi-glaze, reduce to desired consistency, and season to taste with salt and pepper. Stir in butter.

3. Serving. Blanch asparagus tips in boiling water for 1–2 minutes, then cut in fourths. Cut tarts in half, place two halves on each plate, and cover with approximately 1–1½ tablespoons sauce. Garnish with asparagus tips and serve immediately.

NOTES

• Tart shells can be purchased from most bakeries and some large grocery chains.

• Demi-glaze can be purchased from many local restaurants.

SIEGFRIED EISENBERGER

Opposite: Monkeyflowers, Comanche National Grasslands
Overleaf: Sunset, Eagles Nest Wilderness

PEACH TART

1 small jar apricot preserves
1 box frozen puff-pastry dough, thawed
6 ripe peaches
6 tablespoons confectioners' sugar
1 cup heavy cream for garnish
6 scoops peach or apricot sorbet for garnish

SERVES: 6
PREPARATION: 20 minutes
COOKING: 10–15 minutes

PREPARATION

Preheat oven to 450 degrees. In small saucepan, heat apricot preserves over low heat. Lay pastry dough flat and cut out 6 circles approximately 6 inches in diameter. Place on baking sheet and prick with fork. With remaining dough, cut ½-inch wide strips and place on edge of dough circles, creating a rim. Gently press along rim. Peel peaches, cut in half, remove pits, and thinly slice each half. Arrange in fan-shaped pattern on top of dough.

Bake for 10 minutes, remove from oven, brush with apricot preserves, and sprinkle with confectioners' sugar. Return to oven for a few minutes, until sugar turns to caramel.

Whip cream until peaks form. Place tarts on individual plates, top with scoop of sorbet, and place dollop of whipped cream to the side.

NOTE

• Pears, apples, or other fruits can also used.

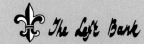

The Left Bank
83 Gore Creek Drive
Vail, Colorado 81657
(970) 476-3696

Born and raised in France, Chef Luc Meyer opened The Left Bank in 1970 and for twenty-five years the restaurant has enjoyed an international reputation. People from around the world return here often for outstanding French cuisine served in a cozy, elegant atmosphere.

LUC MEYER

Recipe is reprinted with permission from author Luc Meyer.

MIXED BERRY GRATIN

Mixed Berries
1 pint fresh strawberries, halved
½ pint fresh blueberries
1 pint fresh raspberries
½ pint fresh blackberries

Sabayon Sauce
⅔ cup sugar
6 egg yolks
½ vanilla bean or
    1½ teaspoon pure vanilla
½ cup milk
1 tablespoon Chambord or
    favorite liqueur

SERVES: 6
PREPARATION: 20 minutes
(refrigerates 3 hours before serving)
COOKING: 25 minutes

Piñons
105 South Mill Street
Aspen, Colorado 81611
(970) 920-2021

Surrounded by turn-of-the-
century paintings depicting the
Wild West, diners are treated
to "American cuisine with
a Colorado touch." Patrons
have been known to fly
across the country for the
elegant food expertly prepared
by Chef Rob Mobilian.

PREPARATION

1. Mixed Berries. Combine berries, divide into six servings, and place on ovenproof plates, refrigerate.

2. Sabayon Sauce. Whip sugar and egg yolks in stainless steel bowl until smooth. Split vanilla bean in half, scrape out insides, combine bean with milk, and bring to a boil in saucepan. Add one fourth of hot milk very slowly to egg mixture, being careful not to "scramble" the eggs. (Adding milk a little at a time allows the temperature of the eggs to increase without cooking.) Whisk eggs, then add remaining milk, stirring continuously.

Return mixture to saucepan and heat, stirring constantly. As soon as the first bubble pops onto surface, remove from heat immediately and transfer to stainless steel bowl. Stir in liqueur. Whip mixture in order to release more heat and cool it down. Refrigerate at least 3 hours.

3. Serving. Preheat broiler. Ladle sauce onto berries and place under broiler until golden brown, 1–2 minutes.

ROBERT MOBILIAN

BLACKBERRY COBBLER WITH GODIVA CUSTARD

Godiva Custard

½ teaspoon unflavored gelatin

2 tablespoons room-temperature water

2 tablespoons packed brown sugar

1 egg, separated

Pinch of salt

¼ cup Godiva liqueur

1 cup heavy cream

Rosemary Pastry

1 cup all-purpose flour

2 teaspoons sugar

1 tablespoon baking powder

½ teaspoon finely chopped
  fresh rosemary

½ teaspoon salt

4 tablespoons unsalted butter

¼ cup heavy cream

Blackberries

3 cups fresh blackberries

¼ cup orange juice

¼ cup plus 2 tablespoons sugar

2 tablespoons cornstarch

2 tablespoons heavy cream

SERVES: 4

PREPARATION: 30 minutes
(custard is refrigerated overnight,
 berries marinate 1½ hours)

COOKING: 20 minutes

Tante Louise
4900 East Colfax Avenue
Denver, Colorado 80220
(303) 355-4488

*Situated in a renovated
Victorian bungalow with
hardwood floors, candlelit
tables, and glowing fireplaces,
Tante Louise is a AAA four-
diamond restaurant. It features
contemporary French-American
fare with an impressive selection
of more than 350 domestic and
imported wines.*

PREPARATION

1. Godiva Custard. Custard should be made 24 hours in advance. Combine gelatin and water in small saucepan, heat gently to dissolve (no warmer than 125–130 degrees), and set aside. Whisk brown sugar, egg yolk, and salt in bowl until light and fluffy; add gelatin mixture and blend well. Stir in Godiva liqueur and set aside. Whisk egg white to medium-peak stage. In separate bowl, whip cream until stiff. Using rubber spatula, gently fold egg white into Godiva mixture, followed by whipped cream. Refrigerate 24 hours.

2. Rosemary Pastry. Heat oven to 400 degrees. Butter 4 1-cup ramekins or 1-quart casserole dish. In large bowl, combine flour, sugar, baking powder, rosemary, and salt. Cut in butter with fork until mixture resembles coarse meal. Stir in cream and mix quickly to form stiff dough. Dust working surface with flour. Roll dough out to ⅜-inch thickness, cut out 4 3-inch circles and set aside.

3. Blackberries. Rinse berries well and drain. Mix with orange juice and ¼ cup sugar and let sit 1½ hours. Stir in cornstarch, mixing well. Divide among ramekins or pour into casserole dish and top with rosemary biscuits. Brush tops with a little cream, sprinkle with 2 tablespoons sugar, and bake 15–20 minutes, or until fruit is thick and bubbly and biscuits are well browned.

4. Serving. Garnish each cobbler with Godiva custard.

MICHAEL DEGENHART

NOTE

• Frozen blackberries can be used when fresh are not available.

RED CHILI AND CINNAMON CHOCOLATE CAKE

1 cup heavy cream

4 tablespoons butter

10 ounces (2½ cups) high-quality
  bittersweet chocolate bits

1½ teaspoons ground cinnamon

1 teaspoon mild red chili powder

5 eggs

⅓ cup sugar

1 teaspoon vanilla

SERVES: 8

PREPARATION: 20 minutes

COOKING: 50 minutes

PREPARATION

Preheat oven to 350 degrees. In medium saucepan, bring cream and butter to a boil. Remove from heat and blend in chocolate, cinnamon, and chili powder, stirring until chocolate melts. Place eggs, sugar, and vanilla in mixing bowl, then set bowl inside larger bowl of hot water. This is called a hot water bath. Whip mixture until warm to the touch. Remove from bath and whip at high speed until triple in volume.

Whisk one fourth of egg mixture into chocolate until well blended. Gently fold in remaining egg mixture until just blended. Pour mixture into buttered and floured 8-inch square cake pan, and bake 50 minutes, or until toothpick inserted in center comes out clean.

Zenith American Grill
1735 Arapahoe Street
Denver, Colorado 80202
(303) 820-2800

Zenith American Grill is home to a new class of western cooking. Chef Kevin Taylor uses regional ingredients and organic vegetables when creating dishes with Asian, Italian, or Southwestern influences. Each plate is a piece of art, presented like a de Kooning canvas.

KEVIN TAYLOR

Aspen trees, San Juan Mountains

CHILLED LEMON SOUFFLÉ WITH RASPBERRY COULIS

Lemon Soufflé
½ envelope unflavored gelatin
2 tablespoons cold water
2 eggs, separated
¼ cup fresh lemon juice
½ cup sugar
1 tablespoons grated lemon rind
½ cup heavy cream

Raspberry Coulis
1 pint fresh raspberries
5 tablespoons sugar
2 tablespoons Grand Marnier or
    similar orange liqueur

PREPARATION

1. Lemon Soufflé. Lightly butter a 1-quart mold. Soften gelatin in water. In double boiler, beat yolks until smooth. Stir in lemon juice, sugar, and lemon rind and cook slowly, stirring until opaque and slightly thickened; stir in gelatin. Set large bowl into larger container filled with ice. Pour lemon mixture into bowl and whisk until cool. In separate bowl, whip cream, then fold into lemon mixture. Whip egg whites until stiff and fold into lemon mixture. Pour into mold and refrigerate at least 4 hours.

2. Raspberry Coulis. Rinse and drain raspberries. In blender or food processor, purée raspberries with sugar and orange liqueur, strain to remove seeds.

3. Serving. Unmold soufflé, place on individual plates, and top with coulis.

NOTE

• The coulis can be made with other fruits and served with fruit soufflés, chocolate tortes, ice cream, etc.

SERVES: 6
PREPARATION: 40 minutes
(soufflé chills for 4 hours)

La Petite Maison
1015 West Colorado Avenue
Colorado Springs, Colorado 80904
(719) 632-4887

Located in a an old Victorian home, La Petite Maison is a small, intimate restaurant where the cuisine is a tender balance of classic cooking and innovative creation. The wine list is as outstanding as the cuisine.

Holly B. Mervis
HOLLY B. MERVIS

LITTLE NELL'S WARM CHOCOLATE CAKE

9 ounces chopped semi-sweet chocolate
¼ cup butter, cut in pieces
2 tablespoons sugar
2 eggs
2 tablespoons all-purpose flour, sifted
Vanilla ice cream for garnish

SERVES: 6
PREPARATION: 20 minutes
COOKING: 15 minutes

PREPARATION

Preheat oven to 400 degrees. In double boiler, melt chocolate and butter, stirring occasionally. Meanwhile, combine sugar and eggs in mixing bowl and beat until thick and doubled in volume. Fold melted chocolate mixture into egg mixture, then fold in flour. Butter or spray 6 ramekins, spoon ½ cup batter in each, and smooth tops. Bake 18 minutes (center will be runny). Let sit 5 minutes. Unmold and serve with vanilla ice cream.

NOTE

• Be sure the melted chocolate doesn't get too hot or it might "scramble" the eggs when mixed in. As a precaution, you might want to stir a small amount of the melted chocolate into the egg mixture first, then fold in the remainder.

THE LITTLE NELL

Restaurant at The Little Nell
The Little Nell
675 East Durant Street
Aspen, Colorado 81611
(970) 920-4600

The Restaurant at The Little Nell combines European ambiance with a Rocky Mountain setting —the ultimate mountain getaway. Chef George Mahaffey mixes regional ingredients with exotic flavors, creating dishes that have won the restaurant Mobil's four-star and AAA's four-diamond awards.

GEORGE MAHAFFEY

Avalanche Creek, Maroon Bells-Snowmass Wilderness

CRÉME BRÛLÉE WITH FRESH RHUBARB

SERVES: 4

PREPARATION: 15 minutes
(chills for 4 hours)

COOKING: 30 minutes

Rhubarb
1 cup plus 2 tablespoons granulated sugar
1 cup plus 2 tablespoons water
1½ cups peeled and diced fresh rhubarb

Crème Brûlée
2 cups heavy cream
2 whole eggs
3 egg yolks
¼ cup granulated sugar
4 tablespoons brown sugar

Mirabelle at Beaver Creek Restaurant

Mirabelle at Beaver Creek
55 Village Road
Beaver Creek, Colorado 81620
(970) 949-7728

Located in a hundred-year-old landmark building, Mirabelle is a nationally acclaimed restaurant. Chef Daniel Joly creates distinctive dishes with a Belgian accent. Homemade pastries and breads, plus an extensive wine list, complement each creation.

PREPARATION

1. Rhubarb. In medium sauce pan, combine sugar and water, bring to a boil, add rhubarb, and continue cooking for 4 minutes. Remove rhubarb from syrup and set aside. Discard syrup.

2. Crème Brûlée. Preheat oven to 325 degrees. In medium saucepan, bring cream to a boil, then remove from heat. Beat whole eggs and egg yolks in bowl and stir in granulated sugar. Add small amount of cream to eggs, whisking continuously. Very slowly add remaining cream, whisking continuously. Be careful not to "scramble" eggs by adding hot cream too quickly.

Place rhubarb in bottom of 4 ramekins, cover with egg-cream mixture, and bake in a warm-water bath (*see Notes*) for 20–25 minutes, or until mixture looks solid. Remove from oven and water bath, and let cool.

3. Serving. Preheat broiler. Sprinkle 1 tablespoon brown sugar evenly over each brûlée, place under broiler until brown sugar bubbles (*see Notes*), then remove from heat, and let cool. Chill for 4 hours.

NOTES

• For the warm-water bath, place the ramekins in a large, shallow pan or casserole dish. Then fill the pan with enough warm water to come halfway up the sides of the ramekins.

• A salamander can be used to create the brown sugar crust. A salamander is a cast iron rod with a round disc at the bottom. The rod is heated and then placed on the brown sugar to form a crust.

DANIEL JOLY

Hazelnut Meringue with Chocolate Ganache and Berries

Hazelnut Meringue
4 egg whites
⅛ teaspoon cream of tartar
5 cups super-fine granulated sugar
1 cup cracked hazelnuts
¼ cup all-purpose flour

Chocolate Ganache
½ pound bittersweet chocolate
1 cup heavy cream
½ cup Frangelica liqueur

Berries
1½ cups assorted fresh berries

Preparation

1. Hazelnut Meringue. Preheat oven to 210 degrees. Whip egg whites in large bowl. As they begin to peak, add cream of tartar and continue whipping until quite stiff. Add sugar and continue whipping for 30 seconds. Fold in nuts and flour.

Using pastry bag, pipe long strips of meringue onto baking sheet covered with oiled parchment paper or wax paper. If pastry bag is not available, use a spoon. Strips should be thin and about the length of the pan. Bake 30–45 minutes, or until meringue is lightly browned and quite crisp. When cool, carefully remove parchment or wax paper and break up into 4- to 6-inch long shards.

2. Chocolate Ganache. In saucepan, heat chocolate, cream, and liqueur over low heat until chocolate melts. Let cool in pan, then transfer to bowl, and whip.

3. Serving. Spoon small amount of ganache onto center of each plate. Arrange meringue shards in ganache so they resemble mountain peaks. Circle with fresh berries.

SERVES: 6
PREPARATION: 45 minutes
COOKING: 45 minutes

KEYSTONE RANCH

Keystone Ranch
1239 Keystone Ranch Road
Keystone, Colorado 80435
(970) 468-4130

The Keystone Ranch is rich in history of the Old West. Ute and Arapaho Indians used the area as their summer campground. Today, guests dine on elegant regional cuisine while seated in a log cabin with views of the Ten Mile and Gore Ranges.

CHRISTOPHER WING

NEGRITAS

1 pound good-quality,
    semi-sweet chocolate

5 egg whites

3 tablespoons Myers' rum

½ cup heavy cream for garnish

PREPARATION

    In double boiler, melt chocolate. Whip egg whites in a stainless steel bowl until stiff and blend into melted chocolate. Blend in rum, ladle into 8 ramekins, and chill for 1–1½ hours. Whip cream until soft peaks form. Top ramekins with whipped cream and serve.

SERVES: 8

PREPARATION: 20–25 minutes
(chills for 1–1½ hours)

COOKING: 25 minutes

The Fort
19192 Route 8
Morrison, Colorado 80465
(303) 697-4771

This unique restaurant, patterned after one of Colorado's first settlement forts, offers the finest in food and drink of the early West. Nestled in the foothills with spectacular views of Denver, The Fort specializes in the unusual, from rattlesnake cocktails to wild Montana huckleberry sundaes.

MICHAEL R. BARNETT

Lupine, Kebler Pass

TIRAMISU

1 cup espresso

2 tablespoons brandy

2 tablespoons Marsala

2 tablespoons coffee extract (optional)

1 package ladyfingers

12 ounces mascarpone cheese

7 ounces prepared vanilla pudding

1¼ cups heavy cream

1 tablespoon sugar

2 pints mixed berries as garnish

PREPARATION

Mix espresso with brandy, Marsala, and 1 tablespoon coffee extract, if using. Line bottom of 6x4-inch loaf pan with half the ladyfingers. Slowly ladle small amount of coffee mixture over ladyfingers. In mixing bowl, combine mascarpone cheese, vanilla pudding, cream, sugar, and remaining coffee extract, if using. Beat until stiff peaks form. Cover ladyfingers with half cheese mixture. Repeat layers one more time, then refrigerate for 6 hours. Slice tiramisu, place one slice on each plate, and circle with berries.

SERVES: 8

PREPARATION: 20 minutes
(chills for 4 hours)

Cliff Young's
700 East Seventeenth Avenue
Denver, Colorado 80203
(303) 831-8900

Cliff Young's is Denver's answer to elegant fine dining. With the romantic, richly decorated Amethyst Room, the stately Crystal Room, or the nonpareil main dining room, Cliff Young's is a truly wonderful epicurean experience.

SEAN BRASEL

DAIRYLESS PUMKPIN PIE WITH WALNUT CRUST

SERVES: 8

PREPARATION: 30 minutes

COOKING: 30 minutes

Terra Bistro
352 East Meadow Drive
Vail, Colorado 81657
(970) 476-6836

Terra Bistro, located in the Vail Athletic Club, takes a holistic approach to dining, offering sophisticated international cuisine prepared with natural ingredients and specializing in free-range meats and poultry. Food is prepared to reduce fat contant while maintaining flavor.

Walnut Crust
¾ cup whole-wheat flour
¾ cup rolled oats
½ cup finely ground roasted walnuts
½ teaspoon ground cinnamon
Pinch of salt
4 tablespoons maple syrup
1 ½ tablespoons water
¼ cup canola oil
Vegetable oil spray

Pie Filling
1 pound tofu
1 cup maple syrup
1 ¾ cups pumpkin purée
1 ½ teaspoons ground cinnamon
⅛ teaspoon ground allspice
¼ teaspoon ground cloves
½ teaspoon ground ginger
½ teaspoon ground nutmeg

PREPARATION

1. Walnut Crust. In large bowl, mix flour, oats, walnuts, cinnamon, and salt. In separate bowl, mix maple syrup, water, and oil. Add wet ingredients to dry and mix lightly. If too dry, add additional water.

Spray tart or pie shell with vegetable oil spray. Press thin layer of nut crust into pan bottom and sides.

2. Pie Filling. Preheat oven to 350 degrees. Purée tofu and maple syrup in blender or food processor. Add pumpkin purée and spices and blend until smooth. Pour into crust and bake 30 minutes, or until top appears set. (The center may still be soft, but it will set completely as it cools.)

CYNTHIA WALT

KAHLUA CHOCOLATE MOUSSE

Mousse
1 cup semi-sweet chocolate bits
⅓ cup Kahlua
1 teaspoon instant coffee
⅓ cup brewed coffee
5 eggs, separated
Pinch of salt

Coffee Whipped Cream
2 cups heavy cream
⅓ cup confectioners' sugar
1 tablespoon instant coffee
1 teaspoon vanilla

PREPARATION

1. Mousse. Melt chocolate in double boiler or stainless steel bowl placed in boiling water. Remove from heat, add Kahlua and instant and brewed coffees, stirring until completely dissolved; mixture should be creamy. In separate stainless steel bowl, whip egg yolks until pale yellow, then slowly add to chocolate. Beat egg whites and salt until stiff; gently fold into chocolate using a spatula. Do not over fold. Pour into 8-ounce cups or glasses, leaving ¾ inch for whipped cream. Cover and refrigerate 4–6 hours.

2. Coffee Whipped Cream. Combine all ingredients in large bowl, beating with mixer at medium speed until cream begins to take on air. Mixture should have consistency of heavy cream.

3. Serving. Pour coffee cream over mousse and serve.

SERVES: 4
PREPARATION: 30 minutes
(chills for 4–6 hours)

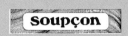

Soupçon
127 A Elk Avenue
Crested Butte, Colorado 81224
(970) 349-5448

Soupçon offers a warm country atmosphere in an intimate setting—there are only nine tables in this gem of the Rockies. Chef-owner Mac Bailey's mission is to "use the freshest ingredients, start from scratch, and make good food."

MAC BAILEY

RECIPES BY RESTAURANT

INDEX

The ratings and information listed in this book were accurate at the time of printing. Please be aware that this information is subject to change.